THE WRITINGS OF ANNA FREUD
Volume VII

PROBLEMS OF PSYCHOANALYTIC TRAINING, DIAGNOSIS, AND THE TECHNIQUE OF THERAPY

1966-1970

THE WRITINGS OF ANNA FREUD
VOLUME VII

PROBLEMS OF PSYCHOANALYTIC TRAINING, DIAGNOSIS, AND THE TECHNIQUE OF THERAPY

1966-1970

INTERNATIONAL UNIVERSITIES PRESS, INC.

NEW YORK

Library of Congress Catalogue Card Number: 67-9514

ISBN 0-8236-6876-2

Manufactured in the United States of America

Preface

This volume contains papers on practical as well as theoretical subjects. To the former category belong some critical reviews on the present arrangements for psychoanalytic training, on the present problematical status of child analysis within the psychoanalytic movement, and, in general, on the pressures and difficulties which beset the members of the International Psycho-Analytical Association at the present time. The latter category is concerned with changes in idea on the concept of the infantile neurosis and its role as forerunner of adult psychopathology; it also brings forward some suggestions referring to a nondescriptive ordering of symptomatology, i.e., a classification on purely metapsychological grounds.

The author hopes that, taken as a whole, the writings contained in this volume will convey a picture of problems in need of solutions and of developments in flux.

Anna Freud

London, 1971

Acknowledgments

The material in this book was collected at the Hampstead Child-Therapy Clinic, an organization which at present is maintained by the Field Foundation, Inc., New York; The Foundation for Research in Psychoanalysis, Beverly Hills, California; the Freud Centenary Fund, London; the Anna Freud Foundation, New York; the Grant Foundation, Inc., New York; the Andrew W. Mellon Foundation, New York; the National Institute for Mental Health, Bethesda, Maryland; the New-Land Foundation, Inc., New York; and a number of private supporters. The author expresses her gratitude for their generous support over many years.

Contents

Part II

Part III

CONTENTS

Part I

1

Problems of Termination
in Child Analysis
(1970 [1957])

We know more, no doubt, about the right time to begin
a child's analysis than we know about the optimum moment for its termination. All that can be presented now,
therefore, are some data and thoughts which open up the
way for further considerations which may lead to greater
certainty in time.

THE DURATION OF TREATMENT IN
CHILD AND ADULT ANALYSIS

When child analysis first appeared on the scene, it was
expected that a child's treatment would be completed more

This paper is in part based on a talk entitled "Termination of
Treatment," which was presented at the Thirty-Fifth Anniversary
of the Youth Guidance Center, Worcester, Mass., on September
20, 1957. Its present version was written in April, 1970. It is here
published for the first time.

quickly than that of an adult. Such optimism was based on the idea that, due to the immaturity of the child's personality, the analyst would be confronted with a less firmly established superstructure in the patient's mind, would have to work through fewer superficial layers before arriving at unconscious content, and that, consequently, the opportunities for interpretation, working through, and the final therapeutic effect would be more quickly reached.

It is common knowledge among analysts by now that these hopes have not been realized. Even though unconscious material and distortions of the ego were more easily revealed, no difference was found in the pace of the curative processes themselves such as the loosening of fixations or reversal of regressions. Also, what is most important from the viewpoint of a child's recovery, the resumption of progressive development proceeds at a slow rate and follows internal laws which refuse to be hurried or accelerated by the analyst's efforts. On the whole, therefore, results in child analysis are not achieved any faster than they are with adults.

PREMATURE TERMINATION IN CHILD ANALYSIS

Every child analyst's fear of failure concentrates on the worry that for one reason or another his young patient's treatment may come to an end prematurely. This concern is a realistic one since most children are worse off after an unfinished analysis than they were before; time, effort, and money have been wasted; the analyst's reputation has been harmed; and, furthermore, the reputation of child analysis itself may suffer a severe setback due to such occurrences.

Since they are not rare (although luckily becoming less frequent), it is well worth the effort to inquire into their causes, which are manifold.

Negative Transference in Relation to Termination

We are past the belief that every period of negative transference in a child's analysis constitutes a definite danger to the continuation of treatment; that children, at such times, either will enter into a battle with their parents about being brought to the analyst's office, or will induce their parents to terminate treatment. We know now that children can work through such phases almost as adults do, and that negative transference manifestations add as much valuable material as they do in adult analysis. Surprisingly, there are even reports on child cases where the negative transference dominated the scene from beginning to end without precluding a successful outcome. This does not mean that child analysts do not interpret negative transference reactions somewhat more promptly than their positive counterparts, to prevent their increasing to quantities which might defy interpretation and carry the patient away from the possibility of any alliance with the analyst. But on the whole, if handled correctly, it is not the negative transference which causes the abrupt ending of otherwise potentially successful analytic child cases.

It is a different matter where those hostile tendencies are concerned which are not displaced from earlier objects to the analyst but evoked by approaches to the child in the analytic hour which we now count among the technical mistakes. Children react adversely whenever ego defenses against unwelcome unconscious content are attacked too suddenly (instead of being drawn into consciousness gradually and considerately), with the result that anxiety is aroused far beyond the quantity with which the child can cope. There are several reports of children who adamantly refused to return to the analyst where this has happened to them.

Other Transference Manifestations in Relation to Termination

On the other hand, transference does not need to be negative to constitute a potential threat to a child's analysis. There are other aspects of it such as quantity or phase-determined quality which may cause the analyst to view it with misgivings.

Some children transfer their *positive* feelings for mother or father to the analyst in a degree which arouses painful loyalty conflicts in them as well as justified jealousy in their parents, both attitudes endangering the continuation of treatment. Where there are no effective parents in the child's home, this excess of transference turns the analyst into too much of a real object for the patient, a development which runs counter to the proper technical use of the transferred manifestations and, again, constitutes a threat to it.

It is a fact, further, that not all the variations of transference are of equal benefit for the analytic process. As I have tried to trace in other contexts,[1] each developmental phase contributes to the transference relationship the specific qualities which are characteristic of it. Thus, transference of oral elements is responsible for the patient's

[1] See *Writings*, Vol. VI.

dependency on the analyst, for his trust in him, but also for the insatiable demandingness which occasionally transcends what can be handled by interpretation. Transference of anal-sadistic strivings accounts for the battles between child and analyst and the ensuing delicate task of freeing as well as of containing the child's aggression in treatment, so as to prevent the analytic process from coming to grief over it. It is only the transferences from the phallic stage which are wholly profitable for the analysis since, besides giving valuable insight (as all the others do), they also provide favorable elements such as cooperativeness, the wish to please, a readiness to give and take, a lessening of ambivalence in relation to the partner, etc.

Our experience has taught us that transference constitutes a threat to the analysis where a child's emotional development has been arrested on the need-fulfillment level (i.e., the level of anaclitic relationships), whether this has been due to a complete lack of adequate mothering from birth onward, or to sudden separations, sudden loss of the mother through death, etc. Not that the anaclitic object relationship does not lend itself to transference onto the analyst. But such relationships are shallow and, above all, egocentric in quality and therefore one-sided. The patient is demanding, insatiable, and intolerant of the ensuing frustration of his transferred wishes. He is unable to stand either the unpleasure or the anxiety aroused by interpretations, or to make any efforts to respond to or work through interpretations. Not to allow treatment of such cases to come to an abrupt and unprofitable end is a most difficult technical task which by implication is as often unsuccessful as it is the opposite.

A transference threat of a different kind arises with fair

regularity in the analysis of adolescents. On the border of preadolescence and adolescence, the so-called adolescent revolt makes its appearance and is almost inevitably transferred onto the analyst. Especially when this has been preceded in treatment by a phase of positive transference, the analyst may be the first object on whom the revolt is lived out. Instead of the young patient breaking away from the parents, or altering the dependent relationship to them, his whole concern may change into the wish to break away from the analysis and the analyst and thereby to gain his independence. At present, we are gathering material and experience in the handling of situations of this nature.[2] Very frequently, though, it is the quantity rather than the quality of the upheaval which determines whether this is legitimate material leading to understanding and relief or whether, in spite of the potential usefulness of the reaction, its magnitude is too much for the analyst to handle and for the patient to endure.

AGREEMENTS AND DISAGREEMENTS CONCERNING TERMINATION IN CHILD ANALYSIS

Ideally, patient, analyst, and parents should decide together on the most profitable moment when a child's analysis has reached termination. In practice, this happy state of affairs does not occur too frequently, and it is well worthwhile to examine the reasons why either one or the other of the partners who have entered into a treatment

[2] [Since this paper was first presented, several reports on this topic have been published. See the references cited in Writings, Vol. V, p. 85.]

contract are either too willing or too unwilling to be dismissed from it.

To include a few figures which have a bearing on this problem: during the three years before this paper was first presented (1954-1957) we terminated forty-nine cases in the Hampstead Child-Therapy Clinic. Of these only seventeen were ended by mutual agreement between patient, therapist, and parent. This leaves us with thirty-two where either the three parties concerned could not agree, or where external rather than internal circumstances brought about termination. In fact, five patients left due to their adolescent revolt against analysis; thirteen treatments had to be ended because of boarding school placement, or because the family left London for another city; eleven child therapists left after their four-year training was completed. As regards length of analysis, the figures are approximate, but an overall estimation shows that the cases terminated by mutual agreement were in analysis for two and three years, while the others averaged one and a half years to two years.[3]

Parents' Reasons for Terminating Analysis

One of the most frequent reasons why parents and analysts disagree about the length of a child's treatment is their different evaluation of manifest *symptomatology*. As an-

[3] Our figures have changed significantly within the last ten or fifteen years, with the increasing technical skill acquired by staff and students. Abrupt termination by the patients has become much rarer. Parents are handled more skillfully and recognize the potential damage done to the child by premature interruption; students frequently remain with us to terminate their cases even if their period of study has been completed.

alysts we know that manifest symptomatology is of questionable value when assessing a child's developmental status or his mental health in general. Also, children can be greatly improved by treatment with their symptoms persisting, or conversely, children's symptoms may disappear without the child being cured. It should not be forgotten, on the other hand, that where parents are not knowledgeable about such matters, they have little or no reason to share the analyst's assessment. They bring the child to treatment, not because of his underlying psychological or developmental disorder, but because of the presenting symptom, not realizing that this is no more than a superficial manifestation of it. Whenever the symptoms disappear, the parents feel justified to put an end to treatment, which in many cases involves them in considerable sacrifices so far as time and effort (even if not money) are concerned. Frequently, they resist as unrealistic the analyst's insistence that therapy is incomplete and should be carried on.

I can quote here by way of illustration a case of school phobia I encountered in my private practice. It concerned the case of a girl of six who greatly alarmed her parents by reacting with attacks of panic when she was supposed to go to school. The parents clamored for an urgent appointment to have this matter treated as soon as possible. But after all arrangements had been made, I received a surprising telephone call from the father. He reported that the child had quieted down and seemed willing to go to school the next day. "In that case," he said, "the mother would, of course, cancel the appointment and they would do their best never to mention the whole incident again." There was no indication that he understood that the refusal to go to school was no more than the surface manifestation of deep underlying anxieties and that it would be worthwhile to relieve the child of these.

But, I suppose there is no reason to be too surprised when meeting parental reactions of this kind. They are all too frequent where breakdowns in toilet training, other phobias, learning disturbances, etc., are concerned.

A very different reason for parents terminating a child's analysis against the therapist's advice is found where the case under treatment is an atypical, autistic or borderline one. We were alerted here to a specific danger, especially with those children who, in spite of severe disturbance and malfunction, seemed to us to present at least limited hope for improvement.

In a number of cases our therapeutic hopes were doomed to disappointment when, sometimes after a very few months, sometimes after a year of efforts from our side, the parents abruptly terminated treatment. Since this always happened after signs of improvement had become visible in treatment, experiences of this kind called for an explanation. We rejected the idea, held in some quarters, that the mother in question needed to have an abnormal child to satisfy some unconscious purpose of her own; or that the family as a whole had adjusted to the child's abnormality to a degree which did not allow for change. Neither of these explanations seemed to us to cover the facts.

What seemed to us much nearer to the true state of affairs is that these atypical and severely retarded children were cases where the mothers had taken infinite trouble to superimpose on the child's abnormality a thin veneer of social adaptation, such as toilet training and some measure of controlled behavior. Even if these were merely the result of mechanical drilling—a type of training which did nothing for the development of the child's personality—it served the circumscribed purpose of allowing the mother to keep the child within the family circle, to mitigate complete rejection of the child by the father, etc. Unfortunately, this rigid pattern of conformity also acted like a strait-jacket within which all further potentialities were confined. Nothing could be done for the child without lifting these restrictions. Nevertheless, lifting them produced as its first effect a former, for the mother highly undesirable, state which was more than she could bear.

An example of this was an atypical, retarded, possibly autistic girl whose speech was restricted to echolalia. She made advances in treatment, used the pronoun "I" for the first time in her life, and began to verbalize her demands on the environment. This step in speech development was accompanied by a general freeing herself of the restrictions imposed on her. She began to soil again, as she had done until the mother had her bowel-trained after a hard struggle. We felt confident that this was no more than a passing phase, that speech might remain and develop further while toilet training would be regained once more. But we could not predict how long the interval would last, and it proved too much for the mother, who broke down under the strain and removed the child.

The Child Analyst's Attitude to Termination of Analysis

Whoever works in a psychoanalytic clinic for children or teaches child analysis in a psychoanalytic institute knows from experience that child analysts are extremely reluctant to terminate their patients' treatment; more than that: that they are frequently under suspicion of delaying termination unduly and in danger of turning every child analysis into an "interminable" one. I have no doubt that such accusations are a serious matter and that they should be investigated as fully as possible to prevent their gaining credence with the general public.

It is a common suspicion held by parents that the analyst, while working with their child, becomes overly attached to him, places himself in the role of father or mother, and delays the ending of treatment so as to delay parting. If this were true it would be a serious matter, certainly, and might well make parents feel extremely reluctant to initiate the whole process of analytic treatment. It is only right to inform all parents that their concerns in this direction are as well known as they are unfounded.

Child analysts (like all analysts) are in personal analysis during the whole four-year period of their training, and this in itself should be sufficient safeguard against any overemotionality in relation to their patients and lead to a constant examination and review of their motivations.

It is true, of course, that all child analysts become fond of their patients during their work with them. But this is hardly different from the situation with other professional workers in the children's field, such as, for example, teachers or hospital nurses. Still, we do not hear of teachers who prevent their pupils from advancing to the next class because they find it too difficult to part with them, or of nurses keeping their patients in bed instead of sending them off home as cured. The only exception here are the nannies in private households who not infrequently kept their charges helpless and dependent so as to assure that they themselves were indispensable to them. But these latter ones were not trained as thoroughly as child analysts are; they were not analyzed, not supervised in their work, not prevented from indulging in acting out their own emotions. I think we can reassure the public that any fully trained child analyst who makes himself or herself guilty of such personal attachments to patients would be quickly disavowed by any reliable institute.

But even with this allegation discarded, there remain several objective reasons why any child analyst should mistrust short treatments, and of course especially abruptly terminated treatments, i.e., why child analyses should take as long as they do at present.

If we go back to the reasons which indicate why a child's analysis is advisable, the answer to the whole question of termination sounds deceptively simple. Children are in urgent need of analytic therapy when normal progressive development is arrested or has been slowed up significantly, whether the reason for this is symptom formation, or excessive defense activity, or undefended anxiety, or massive regression, etc. From this follows that they should be considered cured as soon as the developmental forces have been set free again and are ready to take over. But appealing as this solution is in theory, in practice it is not at all easy to determine when precisely this welcome change in the child's personality is taking place and where exactly in his structure it is operating.

There are many parts to a child's person. The analyst may have been successful in undoing a significant libidinal regression so that thereby the child is helped to reach a formerly abandoned libidinal position. This does not necessarily imply that all the changes which have taken place in his ego organization are undone simultaneously and that his total response on a higher level is assured. Or analysis may have been successful in mitigating the crippling effect of excessive defense activity (such as reaction formations of obsessional strength); this makes a subdued child come to life again, frees his aggressive activity, frequently his learning powers, etc. But, if not helped by the continuation of therapy, this welcome move may be short-lived and give way to new even more unproductive defense activity, or to behavior which is, if anything, further removed from progressive adaptation to the environment.

There also are other and even graver issues to be weighed against each other in the analyst's mind when the question of terminating treatment first appears on the horizon. The child in therapy may be a little boy who, because of excessive castration anxiety, has regressed from the phallic to the anal-sadistic level and after the regression has adopted one of two possible solutions: either to accept his diminished, passive, cruel, dirty, inactive, provocative, emasculated self, or to defend strenuously against it with the help of mechanisms such as repression, reaction formations, conscientiousness, cleanliness, pity, etc. Either solution inhibits further development, of course, and has to be resolved as the consequence of analysis when, with luck, the child can be restored to his parents as the masculine little boy which he had promised to be before the disturbance set in. The parents, certainly, cannot be blamed if they feel satisfied with this result and remove the child.

On the other hand, can we as analysts be blamed if we raise some further doubts and questions? We know from experience that castration anxiety is no simple matter and, in many cases, is superimposed over the castration wishes which are the expression of a boy's inherent passive femininity. Progress may be restarted when the positive oedipus complex has been analyzed; but there remains the uncertainty whether it will proceed unhindered where we have not also uncovered the negative oedipal strivings which underlie it, even if they have not been the active agents in producing the disturbance for which the child has been taken into therapy.

The problem with which we are confronted in this instance also governs all those other cases where threats to normal progress are located either in earlier phases of development or in deeper layers of the personality. The fact that in this area parents and therapists disagree on when to terminate is obviously due to the parents having their eye on the manifest factors whereas the analysts have the hidden, latent, potentially pathological agents in mind.

But analysts also have good reasons against any undue prolongation of the therapeutic process. While pressure is taken off the child during the treatment and drive development profits, the defensive activity of the ego is not helped by the therapy after the initial undoing of excessive and therefore crippling defense activity. Once this is accomplished, we became aware of the fact that we are quite ignorant concerning the ways in which the child will deal with his revived impulses after treatment is completed. Defense activity is, as it were, suspended during the analysis, partly because these processes habitually work in the dark and respond badly to constant exploration and uncovering, partly because the constant attempt to analyze fantasies and undo defenses disturbs their being built up into constructive coping mechanisms. This is a difficulty which becomes obvious quite especially at the border between the first childhood period and the latency phase. We may see a child making moves toward latency during analysis, but usually this phase does not gain dominance before the child's ego is on its own again. This may involve us in many errors when we assess a child's ability to manage by himself after essential recovery.

Now to turn back to the further reasons why child analysts are not in a hurry to dismiss their patients.

During treatment, the child analyst invariably becomes a very important figure in the life of the child and owes this position not only to the transference which has set in and in the course of which the child displaces onto him many of the past and present reactions to his parents which by rights belong to the interplay with them. As explained elsewhere (Vol. VI), he is also a "real" person in the child's life, an adult to be trusted, admired or revolted against, an object for identification, a powerful figure, frequently more powerful than the parents, and—even where there is no intention to take up this role—a guide in the direction taken by the child's development.

When treatment is finished, these latter functions revert altogether to the child's parents irrespective of the fact whether or to what degree they are able to fulfill them.

We have a right to conclude that parents whose child needed treatment in the first instance have either not measured up to the task of upbringing and guiding their offspring or have been faced with pathological constellations of a magnitude with which no normally equipped parent can be expected to cope. In either case the child will remain vulnerable even after a therapeutic success and perhaps need more than the normal amount of careful handling. The therapist who hands over the child to the home surroundings once more and steps out of the situation may doubt, not without reason, what will happen to his patient and whether perhaps injudicious handling will destroy the effects of his analytic efforts; the younger the child, the greater is this concern—hence the hesitation. But the child analyst simultaneously harbors legitimate doubts whether the further safeguarding (i.e., educational guiding) of his former patient really falls within his role. So far, nobody has spelled out what kind of aftercare, if any, should follow child analysis, and if so, who would be the right person to take it over.

DIFFERENT CONCEPTIONS CONCERNING THE ROLE OF CHILD ANALYSIS

There are other open questions concerning the problem of termination which are rooted in the very ideas and conceptions underlying child analysis. Not everybody looks at the latter with the same eyes.

I want to begin here with a plea to child analysts not to forget the distinction between earliest personality development on the one hand and mental disorder on the other. It has become the ambition of the analyst to disregard increasingly the manifest conflicts and to dive down to the very roots of the personality, i.e., to the first year of life when the antecedents of later personality traits are laid down. In embarking on this task, which by its nature prolongs the duration of child analysis, the analyst may get involved in attempts to reverse early processes, only to find that they are irreversible. In my opinion these earliest environmental influences on the child create states which are comparable to the deficiency illnesses on the physical side. While the effects of such early deprivation can be mitigated by later favorable influences, they cannot be undone or reversed or solved in a new more age-adequate way, as conflicts can: this means that they are not in the true sense of the word a legitimate object of analytic effort. What the analyst's work encounters here is a transitional stage between a first settling of the structure and the onset of the intersystemic conflicts out of which the infantile neurosis will arise.

We might also formulate it differently: whenever the child analyst transcends the area of the infantile neurosis or of the neurotic conflicts preceding it, he finds himself in the area of the "basic faults" (M. Balint, 1958)—the arrests, the irregularities of development, i.e., the non-neurotic childhood disorders—where his analytic efforts may well become interminable ones.

There are other conceptions of child analysis which not everyone looks at with the same eyes. For some analysts, child analysis is no more than an extension of the area to which the analytic therapy can be applied, i.e., to immature instead of to mature human individuals.

In contrast to this, others are interested in child analysis above all as a method of prevention, i.e., a technique to nip potential pathology in the bud, long before it has hardened into phenomena which are either difficult or impossible to reverse and dissolve. Others again are of the opinion that no pathology, even if it exists merely as a potentiality, is needed to indicate the application of analysis for a child; that, in fact, child analysis is a powerful instrument that helps shape an individual child's personality and is needed as an extension to the more conventional forms of upbringing. As such it has to be longlasting and accompany the child through the developmental hazards, seek to undo fixations even before they have had the time to become established, prevent regressions—in short, deal on every level of development with the potential residues that might constitute hindrances to smooth progress in the future. We may be justified in saying that whoever views child analysis in this light will not be content to see it end before the developmental process itself has reached its aim and maturity has been achieved.

Each individual child analyst will have to examine his own attitude toward these different evaluations of the process and choose his own stand. There are many of us who are unwilling to subscribe to the extreme claims of the last-named group and reserve for child analysis the status of a therapeutic and preventive measure only. And even as regards prevention we are well advised to guard against extreme optimism. It is true that children who have undergone analytic therapy to relieve them of the crippling effect of an infantile neurosis may in some ways be better equipped than others to deal with stresses which arise at later stages. On the other hand, the advantages gained by a child in analysis may be offset by the scars which every illness leaves. To include here a comparison with what happens on the physical side: patients who have recovered from a severe illness early in life may, in some cases, have acquired a degree of immunity; others are certainly not favored over those who were never subject to a manifest illness and are then left by it more sensitive and vulnerable than they would have been without it.

Above all, experience teaches us that each developmental phase contains specific hazards which are characteristic of it; that environmental stresses and traumata are unpredictable; and that no successful conflict solution on one level can act as safeguard and immunization against the conflicts and difficulties in store for the individual in the future.

Notwithstanding these arguments, there is some evidence that even those of us who are modest in our demands on the achievements of child analysis are not altogether unmoved by its more ambitious aspects. We agree, after all, that analysis, at whatever age it is applied, is a powerful instrument in altering the basic configuration of a personality. We agree, further, that deviations from the norm, whether in the area of the drives or of the ego, are more easily influenced before they have become ingrained. We know that whatever happens at an early level will alter and distort (or set right) what happens at a later one. There is no doubt that these aims are in the background of our minds even if therapy, i.e., the relief from pathological pressure in the present, is our avowed aim. All these implied ambitions cannot be accommodated unless the therapeutic process itself is given ample time to unfold itself. Thus, whatever our theoretical stand may be, none of us will with a good conscience vote for any shortening of analytic treatment. Rather, summing up the termination problem we would say: there may be a few children whom we keep too long in treatment, but they do not compare in number with those whom we do not treat long enough.

2

A Discussion with
René Spitz
(1970 [1966])

An exchange of ideas between René Spitz and myself is long overdue and, in fact, there is hardly any area in either his or my publications which does not provide a profitable opening for such a task. In what follows, I select from these some points of agreement, some of disagreement, as well as some which offer opportunities for further discussion and for mutual stimulation.

This paper is based on a lecture presented on the occasion of the seventy-ninth birthday of René A. Spitz, which was celebrated by the Swiss Psycho-Analytical Association, Zurich, January, 1966. First published under the title, "Eine Diskussion mit René Spitz," *Psyche*, 21:4-15, 1967. The English version, written in 1970, is here published for the first time.

BASIC ASSUMPTIONS, AREAS OF
WORK, METHODS

So far as agreements are concerned, René Spitz and I share the theoretical assumptions on which his as well as my work is based, a conformity of scientific outlook which extends beyond the mere fact that we are both psychoanalysts. Within the framework of psychoanalytic psychology, we both adhere firmly to a belief in the fundamental significance of the pleasure-pain principle as a regulatory factor in the life of the infant. We both maintain that it is unsatisfactory to describe any phenomenon occurring in the child—whether this is a particular mode of behavior, a detail of his experience or development—from one angle only, that is to say, either from the point of view of drive development or that of ego development or that of object relations. We share the conviction that psychoanalytic, i.e., metapsychological, thinking needs to encompass all the different aspects, which means that psychological phenomena have to be examined in terms of their genesis, dynamics, economics, structure, and their significance for adaptation to the external world.

So far as areas of work are concerned, we have come fairly close together, even though our starting points were rather far apart. René Spitz was from the outset attracted to unravel what occurs in the mind of the infant during the first year of life. We find his interest most deeply engaged when he is confronted with the immature human organism, standing at the threshold of differentiation, structuralization, and acquisition of language. In contrast to this, my interest has taken the opposite course, downward not upward the developmental ladder, i.e., from latency and adolescence to the phallic period of the infantile neurosis, and only from there to the early determinants of personality formation. We met finally at the border between the first and second year of life, at the point where the transitions from pleasure principle to reality principle and from primary process to secondary process functioning can be observed most clearly.

As regards methods of exploration, we share the conviction that for early childhood direct observation of manifest behavior is an important tool and supplements the data which can be elicited from the analyses of adults and older children. This does not mean that we underestimate the merits of the reconstructive method. There is no doubt for us that the most important constituents of psychoanalytic child psychology were discovered during the analyses of adults; examples are such basic findings as the succession of libidinal phases, the details of the oedipus and castration complexes, infantile amnesia, etc. In spite of these unquestioned achievements, we do not think that reconstruction from later analysis is sufficient to provide full insight into the earliest developmental processes, especially where ego development is concerned. There is the danger that one might rely too heavily on the observation of the regressive functioning which is induced and promoted by the analytic treatment situation, forgetting that these regressive manifestations inevitably include later acquisitions. Where the imprint of more highly developed functions is superimposed on the remnants of archaic layers, the original simplicity of the primitive picture cannot but be distorted; this is true in particular where regression proceeds from verbal to preverbal phases, as it happens in the transference situation. René Spitz and I both feel that with regard to the study of the first eighteen months of life, direct observation is indispensable as a means to complement, correct, and verify the conclusions drawn from the analyses of later stages.

On the other hand, it is also in the area of methodology that René Spitz and I are far apart. Where he sets up experiments, I engage in so-called action research, i.e., activities which are geared to educational, or humanitarian, or therapeutic aims, the observations coming in as a by-product. While he employs academically trained assistants, I have always used in addition practical workers such as children's and hospital nurses, nursery school teachers, etc. While his researches follow a preconceived plan, I use as the basis of my investigations, apart from the analytic findings, also the accidental and fortuitous happenings as they occur in everyday life.

There are, probably, advantages and disadvantages inherent in both of these procedures. Spitz may claim that an observational method loses value if the observer interferes actively with the phenomena he observes. I may claim, in reply, that action research has two significant assets of its own: while experiments are set up for stated minutes, at best hours, our type of observation extends over whole days or weeks, in some instances on a twenty-four-hour basis; also it seems to me that only action research deals with the natural phenomena of life in their full extent and meaning. What unfolds before the eyes of the observer under these circumstances are not circumscribed reactions but the whole gamut of pain, anxiety, jealousy, envy, anger, hostility, aggression, love, passion, curiosity, etc., which together convey an impressive picture of the internal happenings as well as of the interactions between the child's internal and external world.

My co-workers and I can further claim as an additional asset that we have access to a source of material not used by Spitz, namely, the therapeutic analyses of very young children to which we owe much important knowledge and the understanding of many minute details of early infantile development. Child analysis is in this respect more than a supplement to the reconstructional method or to direct observation: it is an independent, invaluable, and inexhaustible source of new insights. Nevertheless, René Spitz would be justified in maintaining that it is not applicable in the first year of life.

We find ourselves in much closer agreement once more when it comes to the question whether the existing methods of psychological testing can be fruitfully integrated with either his or my work. René Spitz, for his part, expresses his dissatisfaction with the fact that these tests do not yield clinical material, do not depict internal experience, and do not inquire sufficiently into the infant's object dependency. While subscribing to these opinions, we, on our part, go a step beyond this by maintaining that psychoanalytic observers might be well qualified to devise their own methods of evaluation, i.e., testing schemes based on metapsychological thinking. We hold out the hope that the Developmental Profile, set up for the diagnostic assessment of older children in the Hampstead Clinic,[1] might be adapted for use with infants in the near future.[2]

[1] See *Writings*, Vol. V, ch. 3; Vol. VI, ch. 4.
[2] See W. E. Freud (1967).

THE DEVELOPMENT OF OBJECT RELATIONSHIPS

I chose as the second subject for discussion the gradual unfolding of object relatedness in the human infant, a topic of overriding importance to both of us. I, together with many other analysts, approach this on the basis of the libido theory and recognize a *prestage* of object relation in which the infant invests with libido the experience of drive or need fulfillment, regardless of the source or agency from which they are derived. We may say that at this point he "loves" nothing except the satisfaction itself and has not yet reached the stage when he will extend his love, i.e., the libidinal cathexis, from the pleasure in satisfaction to the person by whom the satisfaction is provided. We have wondered frequently what facilitates the latter transition, and this is a point where Spitz's findings and the conclusions drawn from them provide most useful additions to existing conceptions. Spitz approaches the topic from the viewpoint of ego psychology, i.e., via the infant's gradual apperception of the Gestalt of the mother's face. He describes in minute detail the maturational steps in the various perceptual processes which finally enable the infant to recognize these crucial Gestalts, first of the maternal face, later of the whole maternal figure. According to him, it is only when this perceptual ability has been acquired that object relatedness itself can be established. For the love of satisfaction the infant needs to perceive only the pleasure-pain processes as they make themselves felt in the internal world; the capacity to love the mother presupposes the additional perception of elements in the external world. Spitz's findings on the ego side and our assumptions derived from the libido theory complement each other at this point and form a harmonious whole.

The same consensus of opinion between us also governs the next stage, that of the *anaclitic* relationship during which the infant now perceives, recognizes, and cathects the mother, even though love still remains based on and maintains itself via the satisfactions provided by her.

No one describes better than Spitz, or more convincingly, the outstanding role that anaclitic love plays for the infant's life and death, in the present as well as in the future. His observations of motherless, i.e., objectless, infants are pioneering investigations, and the concept of "anaclitic depression" which he introduced, has become an undisputed part of psychoanalytic child psychology and childhood psychopathology. He demonstrated the function of the anaclitic object for the early fusion of love and hate and their turning toward the outside world, and described the pathological consequences of its absence when aggression and hatred remain within the self. I only need to quote his prognostic statement: "Infants without love . . . will end as adults full of hate" (1965, p. 300).

While subscribing wholeheartedly to these conclusions, I want to add some considerations which are derived from reconstructions in child analysis and adult analysis and alert us to the fact that additional to its positive aspects, the anaclitic phase also harbors certain dangers for future development. Human individuals may become arrested at this stage; or they may acquire a fixation point here to which their libido is apt to regress from later, more mature constellations. In either case such persons show infantile patterns in their love life. Instead of relating to their partners on the mature level of object constancy, give and take, loyalty, and consideration for the other's personal qualities and attributes, they relate, as infants do, selfishly and egoistically, motivated by demands and needs, intolerant of frustration, and with promiscuity, i.e., they immediately search for a new object where not enough satisfaction is forthcoming. So far we are still uncertain whether it is only excessive frustration in the first year of life or also excessive gratification which leads to this pathological and unwelcome outcome. Excessive gratification in the anaclitic phase may have the consequence that all later forms of relationship are in essence disappointing, i.e., constitute a decrease of pleasurable experience. On the other hand, lack of satisfaction in the early stage may give rise to a compulsory search for compensation and the inability to make any libidinal investment in animate or inanimate objects except according to the anaclitic, i.e., need-satisfying model. There may be a path leading from this to the understanding of the addictions to alcohol, drugs, etc.

There are a number of other developments which lead from the anaclitic type of love to other aspects of the mother-child relationship. Spitz has devoted his life's work to their clarification and his writings in this area are as extensive as they are intensive.

One aspect that has attracted his attention is the difference in the libidinal development of children who have only a *single early object,* the mother, and those who are raised by a *multitude of caretaking adults,* as is inevitably the case in residential institutions. In this respect, each of his findings can be corroborated by confirmatory evidence from me and my co-workers. We have had ample opportunity to follow the development of motherless children and of children brought up in groups, and were made keenly aware of the peculiar changes that result from such deviations from the normal fate of children. As an example of such a deviation I mention the fact that twins, even when they are raised by their own mother, do not develop a mother-child relationship in the normal and natural way. A twin has from the very beginning of his life not one object but two: his mother and his twin. From the start he also has a rival in his mother relationship with whom he must share the earliest satisfactions. As a consequence, neither the anaclitic type of love nor the first object love develops under normal conditions, a circumstance that results in the peculiarities of the personality development of twins, as we saw in our War Nurseries (see Burlingham, 1951).

We saw different deviations from normal development in the children rescued from concentration camps.[3] In their case, the *complete absence of the mothers*, the lack of any family, and the constant change of nurses were the factors that induced these children to form attachments not to adults but to the group members of their own age. The results appeared not only in changes in their love life and the absence of normal affects such as jealousy and rivalry; there were also far-reaching alterations in their identifications and the superego formation based on them. I agree with René Spitz that it is worth the effort to study such exceptional fates and to draw conclusions from them concerning the role that the mother normally plays in the life of the child.

Spitz (1965) quotes Freud's statement that "the original helplessness of human beings is . . . the primal source of all

[3] See *Writings*, Vol. IV, ch. 8.

moral motives" (1895, p. 379), and expands it in a special way: he views the infant's relation to his mother as the primal source of the most important functions, affects, and attitudes—in short, as the primal source of becoming a human being. He describes how the existence of the mother, her mere presence, stimulates the infant; how their interchanges influence perception, affects, and the need to communicate; and how only this interchange between two human beings beginning in the earliest periods of life guarantees that the asocial infant develops into a member of the human community. Spitz convinces us that many aspects of the mother-child relationship which we as analysts usually place in later stages should be ascribed to the first year of life. He depicts the mother in her inhibiting as well as in her encouraging role, in her function as source of stimulation and imitation, as the first object of identification, etc.

For my part, I have described in which way the role of the mother as the *first legislator* in the life of the infant is of special interest. On the basis of the mother's regulation of the infant's need gratification—i.e., the alternation of pleasure and pain, the fulfillment and refusal of wishes— the child learns for the first time to appreciate the full impact of the external world and forms his first reactions to it. We see that some infants submit more or less willingly to the restrictions imposed by the mother, while others are enraged and cry in protest and insist on the fulfillment of their wishes. What we are here confronted with may perhaps be a first forerunner of the older child's and adult's subsequent attitude to rules and laws and to the instinctual renunciation imposed on the individual by society (see Vol. VI).

Spitz views each *individual characteristic of the mother* as representing a factor in the external world of the child. The interaction of child and mother has therefore the same significance for him as the interaction between internal and external world.[4]

Spitz objects, as I do, to speaking of "good" and "bad" mothers, a habit that has persisted through many decades, especially in the field of social work.[5] Interestingly enough, the concept of the good or the bad mother also keeps reappearing in our reconstructions from adult analyses. The analytic process requires us to view the past as our patients do and to identify ourselves with their affects. In the patient's recollection and in his transference he says that mother is "good" when she gratifies, and "bad" when she frustrates. Such estimates, however, stem from a period of life when the pleasure-pain principle ruled supreme and precluded evaluations by any other yardstick. We must not forget that such estimates are subjectively founded; they are not objective and are incapable of doing justice to the innumerable variations and complexities in a mother's conduct. I would assume that Spitz's book, *The First Year of Life*, accomplishes what I was unable to achieve, namely, put an end to such unwarranted oversimplifications.

That the mother-child relationship is of necessity *asymmetrical* is a further point stressed by René Spitz and one that other authors are inclined to underestimate. Spitz shows how unequal the contributions are that mother and

[4] See also Augusta Bonnard's frequently repeated statement: "The psychic reality of the mother is the external reality of the child."

[5] See my discussion of the concept of the "rejecting" mother (*Writings*, Vol. IV, ch. 29).

child make to their symbiotic union. At the beginning of life the infant is passive, the mother is active. Later, conditions are reversed: the child is active and the mother is passive. As an adult the mother is a highly differentiated being, while the infant is still undifferentiated. The mother lives in a social community to which she is adapted in innumerable ways. The infant has a relationship to only one person, the mother, who assumes the role of representing the entire external community for him. It is not surprising that a partnership between two such unequal beings leads to many upsets and conflicts.

Again, I insert here one further consideration, namely, that such differences between mother and child are particularly noticeable in the area of libidinal cathexis. In normal circumstances the mother has many objects (husband, other children, parents, friends, etc.); the child has at the beginning only one object, the mother, from whom he expects the same exclusive relationship. As we know from analyses of adults and from direct observations of children, this original exclusiveness gives rise to early infantile jealousy, to the child's libidinal dissatisfaction, to his feeling inferior, i.e., not sufficiently valued and loved. We are familiar with the harmful consequences of these early disappointments in love. On the other hand, we know of children whose divorced or widowed mothers concentrated all their libido on the child as their only love object, and we are convinced that the emotional situation resulting from these circumstances is equally unhealthy. The asymmetry of the mother-child relationship is obviously a normal condition of life, painful as it may be to the infants themselves.

There is only one point in this area where I find myself

unable to subscribe to Spitz's views. He goes further than most in ascribing specific psychosomatic disorders of the infant to specific emotional disorders of the mother. My objections to this assumption rest on two arguments: one, that the complex personalities of the mothers are insufficiently assessed, namely, by observational methods only, not on the basis of their analysis; two, that according to my beliefs, no childhood disorder is due to environmental influence alone but always to the interaction between external and internal factors, i.e., in this instance, the impact of a mother's personality on the constitutional givens in the child, the latter being variable from case to case.[6]

THE INFANTILE TRAUMA

A further, almost irresistible subject for discussion is that of the incidence of traumatic experiences in infancy, even though it can hardly be dealt with in this framework doing justice to all its complexities and ramifications.

As analysts we maintain that the impact of a pathogenic influence is all the greater, the earlier in life it occurs, an assumption which is in direct opposition to Spitz's statement with regard to the first year of life: "I cannot emphasize sufficiently how small a role traumatic events play in this development" (1965, p. 139). However, what appears at first glance as an irreconcilable clash of opinions reveals itself on closer inspection as a mere difference in terminology which obscures a remarkable similarity in thinking about the psychic processes in question.

Freud's original concept of trauma as a breach of the

---

[6] See also my Preface to Spitz's book (1957, 1965).

stimulus barrier due to excessive stimulation from either the internal or external world has undergone extensive changes in the course of years. Even in Freud's own writings we find, in addition to the shock trauma, the concept of the retrospective trauma, i.e., an experience that acts traumatically not at the time of its occurrence but only retroactively in memory. Then in more or less rapid succession were added the "strain trauma" (E. Kris, 1956), i.e., an experience that becomes traumatic by overtaxing the resources of the psychic apparatus; the "cover trauma" (E. Kris, 1956; A. Freud, *Writings*, Vol. IV, ch. 7), which is to be conceived of in analogy to cover memories; the "silent trauma" (W. Hoffer, 1952), which exerts its influence especially in the inner world of the young infant without manifesting itself in the outside world by means of noisy symptoms; the "cumulative trauma" (Khan, 1963), which achieves traumatic impact only by virtue of the constant repetition of a pathogenic stimulus; the "secondary trauma" (Sandler, 1967); the "constructive trauma" (R. Waelder, 1967); the trauma that exerts its impact not through the quantity of stimulation but through the quality of experience (Greenacre, 1967).

This broadening of the definition of trauma, extending the term beyond its original, purely economic significance, has by no means contributed to the clarification of this concept. The individual author has a difficult task finding his way through this area and today is in danger of calling a trauma everything that in one form or another exerts a pathogenic influence on the mental life of a person.

I have tried to counteract this danger by reverting to the economic conception of trauma and by relating it to our views of the significance of a functioning ego (see Vol. V, ch. 14). In this way I arrive at the definition of trauma as any event in the internal or external world that owing to its suddenness, quantity or quality of excitation is capable of putting the ego out of action for brief or prolonged periods of time. When this happens and the individual is deprived of all ego functions and defensive operations, he will react to the experience by resorting to primitive, archaic, and frequently somatic responses. Instead of using defenses such as denial, repression, projection, etc., he has recourse to reaction patterns which belong to an era before the psychic apparatus was differentiated into id and ego agencies. This produces panic states in the place of anxiety signals; motor paralysis or chaotic motility in the place of appropriate motor activity; futile repetitiveness instead of purposeful abreaction or working through; etc.

If we adopt this view of trauma, we acquire simultaneously two useful criteria for assessing its severity. One concerns the length of time during which the ego remains out of action. The second concerns the quality of functioning after the ego has resumed its role. We would regard the trauma as a severe one if the ego has been paralyzed longer than momentarily and if, after resumption of ego activity, functioning remained either temporarily or permanently on a regressed level.

It is obvious that viewed from this theoretical aspect, Spitz's rejection of the concept of infantile trauma assumes a very different meaning. If one defines trauma in terms of the ego, i.e., as damage done to the ego organization, then the concept is not applicable to a developmental stage before id and ego have become differentiated from each other. What can be endangered at this time of life is ego development rather than a not yet existing ego functioning. Processes such as the domination of life by primary process functioning, by the repetition compulsion, by the occurrence of panic states are not exceptions, as they will be later; they are the rule. Even if the neonate is considered protected against excessive stimulation by a high threshold of excitation, the older infant may be thought of as potentially traumatized all the time since his rudimentary ego has no ability to cope with overstimulation from either external or internal sources. What comes to his rescue normally are the ministrations of his mother who, by providing care, protection, and comfort, assumes the role of a protective shield, holds off external excitations, and alleviates internal stimuli. It is only in the second year of life that this function of the protective shield (or auxiliary ego) gradually passes over from the mother to the child himself and is taken over by his own ego.

It becomes a fairly easy task here to relate, or even to translate, Spitz's expositions concerning the "affective climate" in infancy into the language of trauma theory. By stressing the importance of constant alternation between stimulation and response in the mother-infant interchanges, he deals with the events which otherwise constitute the "silent" traumatizations of the child. By emphasizing the pathological consequences when the infant is deprived of the mother's attention and protection, he deals with the "shock" trauma. Since he affirms his belief in the far-reaching effect of constantly repeated adverse happenings, he is not far from discussing the "cumulative" trauma. We might even attribute to him some concurrence with the concept of a "constructive" trauma since he shares with us the belief that it is the painful experience of helplessness when confronted with powerful stimulation which induces the child's ego gradually to learn to exercise and to assume the functions of the stimulus barrier.

To say it in other words: it may be legitimate to assume that all the variations and separate constellations of the infantile trauma listed above are already contained in Spitz's concept of the reciprocal interaction between mother and child.

3

Adolescence as a Developmental Disturbance (1969 [1966])

Within this Congress symposium there is no time for more than broad statements of the views which we, as speakers, hold with regard to adolescence. There is the scope neither for presenting the evidence for the positions which we adopt nor for adding the clinical illustrations which make theoretical statements come to life. Nevertheless, I cannot help taking some minutes off for an attempt to place the adolescent reactions where I imagine them to belong, namely, at an intermediary point on the line between mental health and mental illness.

Presented at the 6th International Congress for Child Psychiatry, Edinburgh, July 25, 1966. First published in *Adolescence: Psychosocial Perspectives*, ed. S. Lebovici & G. Caplan. New York: Basic Books, 1969, pp. 5-11.

THE PSYCHOANALYTIC VIEW OF MENTAL HEALTH AND ILLNESS

Our psychoanalytic investigations of individuals have convinced us that the line of demarcation between mental health and illness cannot be drawn as sharply as had been thought before. Especially so far as the neuroses are concerned, neurotic nuclei are found in the minds of normal people as regularly as large areas of normal functioning are part of the makeup of every neurotic. Moreover, people cross and recross the border between mental health and illness many times during their lives.

There is the further point that the concept of health as it has been developed in the physical field cannot be taken over to the mental side without alteration. Physically, we are healthy so long as the various organs of the body function normally and, via their specific functioning, contribute to an overall state of well-being. Mentally, more than this is needed. There, it is not sufficient if each part of the mind as such is intact since the various parts of our personality pursue different aims, and since these aims are only too often at cross-purposes with each other. Thus, we may be healthy so far as our instinctual drives are concerned; or our sense of reality plus adaptation to the environment may be well up to mark; or our ideals may be considered admirable by other people. Nevertheless, these single items do not yet add up to the result of mental health. The latter is produced only where all the agencies in our mind, drives, reasonable ego, and ideals coincide sensibly and in adaptation to the external world resolve the conflicts inherent in the total situation. To say it in different words: mental health depends on workable compromises and on the resulting balance of forces between the different agencies and different demands.

THE CONCEPT OF DEVELOPMENTAL DISTURBANCES

It is implied in the above view that this balance and these compromises are precarious and apt to be upset by any alteration in the internal or external circumstances. It is also obvious that such changes are as inevitable as they are continuous, and that they occur especially frequently on the basis of development. Every step forward in growth and maturation brings with it not only new gains but also new problems. To the psychoanalyst this means that change in any part of mental life upsets the previously achieved balance and that new compromises have to be devised. Such change may affect the instinctual drives, as happens in adolescence; or it may occur in the ego, i.e., in the agency whose function it is to manage or control the drives; or what undergoes change may be the individual's demands on himself, his aims and ideals; or his love objects in the external world; or other circumstances in his environment. Changes may be qualitative or quantitative. Whatever they are, they alter the internal equilibrium.

Developmental disturbances of this kind may be observed, for example, in the area of sleep and food intake in early childhood. Infants may be perfect sleepers at the beginning of life, i.e., drop off to sleep whenever they are tired and no stimulus from inside or outside their bodies is strong enough to disrupt their peace. This will alter with the normal further mental developments when the child's clinging to the people and happenings in the environment make it difficult for him to withdraw from them and turn falling asleep into a conflictual process. Likewise, the disturbing food fads of childhood are no more than the impact on eating of various infantile fantasies of dirt, of impregnation through the mouth, of poisoning, of killing. These fantasies are tied to various specific phases of development and therefore transitory, as are the feeding disturbances based upon them. In fact, in the clinical practice with children, the concept of transitory developmental disturbances has become indispensable to us as a diagnostic category.[1]

It is worth mentioning here that developmental change not only causes upset but can also bring about what is called spontaneous cures. A case in point here are the temper tantrums which serve young children as affective motor outlets at a time when no other discharge is available to them. This is altered by the mere fact of speech development which opens up new pathways and by which the former turbulent and chaotic behavioral manifestation is rendered redundant.

THE ADOLESCENT REACTIONS AS PROTOTYPES OF DEVELOPMENTAL DISTURBANCES

I return to the problems of adolescence which, in my view, are the prototypes of such developmental disturbances:

While in the childhood disorders of this nature we are usually confronted with alterations in one or the other area of the child's personality, in adolescence we deal with

[1] [See especially Writings, Vol. V, ch. 3; Vol. VI; and Nagera, 1966.]

changes along the whole line. There are, as a basis, on the physical side, the alterations in size, strength, and appearance. There are the endocrinological changes which aim at a complete revolution in sexual life. There are changes in the aggressive expressions, advances in intellectual performance, reorientations with regard to object attachments and to social relations. In short, the upheavals in character and personality are frequently so sweeping that the picture of the former child becomes wholly submerged in the newly emerging image of the adolescent.

Alterations in the Instinctual Drives

So far as the sexual drive in adolescence is concerned, I have found it useful to differentiate between quantitative and qualitative changes. What we observe first, in the period of preadolescence, is an indiscriminate increase in drive activity which affects all the facets which have characterized infantile sexuality, i.e., the sexual-aggressive responses of the first five years of life. At this time the preadolescent individual becomes, as a first step, hungrier, greedier, more cruel, more dirty, more inquisitive, more boastful, more egocentric, more inconsiderate than he has been before.[2] This escalation of the infantile elements is then followed, shortly thereafter, by a change in quality of the drives, namely, by the changeover from pregenital to genital sexual impulses. This new element involves the adolescent in a type of danger with which he is not accustomed to deal. Since, at this stage, he still lives and functions as a member of his family unit, he runs the risk

[2] [For a more detailed description of this developmental phase, see *Writings*, Vol. IV, ch. 5.]

of allowing the new genital urges to connect with his old love objects, i.e., with his parents and siblings.

Alterations in the Ego Organization

It is the temptation of becoming involved, first in sexual-aggressive pregenital behavior and, following this, in incestuous fantasies which causes all those alterations in the ego that impress the observer as the adolescent's personal upheaval and also as his unpredictability. Serious attempts are made to keep the quantitative drive increase under control as it has been controlled in former times. This is done by means of a major effort on the side of the defenses. This means bringing into play more repressions, more reaction formations, more identifications and projections, and in some individuals even more determined attempts at intellectualization and sublimation. It also means that the entire defensive system of the ego is overstrained and that therefore the frantic warding off of impulses alternates with breakthroughs of drive activity. When we approach a young adolescent, we never know which of these two aspects we are going to meet: his overstrict, inhibited, highly defended personality or his infantile, openly aggressive, openly sexual, unrestrained primitive self.

Alterations in the Relation to Objects

What serves the adolescent in some manner as a protection against the quantitative pressure of the drives proves wholly ineffective against the changeover to the primacy of the genital urges, i.e., adult sexuality proper. Nothing helps here except a complete discarding of the people who were important to him as love objects in his past, namely, of his parents. This struggle against the parents is carried out in a variety of ways: by openly displayed indifference toward them, i.e., by denying their importance; by disparagement of them, since judging them as stupid, useless, ineffective people should make it easier to do without them; by open insolence and revolt against the beliefs and conventions which were previously shared with them. That all this also alternates with throwbacks to helplessness and dependence does not make it any easier for the parents themselves. Obviously, the task demanded from them is a double one: to be self-effacing, thick-skinned, and reserved at one time, and to change over at a moment's notice to being sympathetic, alert, helpful as in former times.

The closer the tie between child and parent has been, the more violent will be the fight against them in adolescence.[3]

Alterations in Ideals and Social Relations

The adolescent's change in social relations follows as the direct consequence of his stepping out of his family. He is not only left without his old object ties; together with the ties to the parents, he has also overthrown the ideals which he formerly shared with them and he has to find substitutes for both.

There is a parting of the ways here which, I suppose, leads to two different patterns in the adolescent culture. Some adolescents put in the place of the parents a self-chosen leader who himself is a member of the parent gen-

[3] [See *Writings*, Vol. II; and Vol. V, ch. 9.]

eration. This person may be a university teacher, a poet, a philosopher, a politician, who is invested with Godlike qualities and followed, gladly and blindly. In our times this solution is comparatively rare. More frequently adopted is the second possibility where the peer group as such, or a member of it, is exalted to the role of leadership and becomes the unquestioned arbiter in all questions of moral and aesthetic values.

The hallmark of the new ideals, as well as of the new emotionally important objects, is their contrast with the former ones. In the remote past when I myself was of adolescent age, there had sprung into being on the European continent the so-called Youth Movement, a first attempt at an independent adolescent culture. This was directed against bourgeois complacency and capitalism, and the ideals upheld by it were those of socialism, intellectual freedom, aestheticism, etc. Poetry and classical music were what the parents did not believe in and the adolescents did. We know how far the tide has turned in the last two generations. At present, the adolescents are hard put to discover new ideals—constructive or disastrous—which can serve to mark the dividing line between their own and their parents' lives.

CONCLUDING REMARKS

To the above abbreviated summary of our main theme, I add a few concluding remarks which concern more general issues.

First, it has always struck me as unfortunate that the period of adolescent upheaval coincides with such major demands on the individual as those for academic achievements in school and university, for a choice of career, for increased social and financial responsibility in general. Many failures, often with tragic consequences, in these respects are due not to the individual's incapacity as such but merely to the demands being presented to him at a time of life when all his energies are engaged in solving other major problems, namely, those created for him by sexual growth and development.

Secondly, I feel that the preponderance of sexual problems in adolescence should not be allowed to obscure the role of aggression which, possibly, might be of great significance. It is worthwhile noting that countries which are engaged in a battle for existence, such as, for example, Israel, do not report the same problems with their adolescents which are prevalent here. The main difference is that the aggression of the adolescent generation is not lived out within the family and the community but directed against the enemy outside of the nation and employed in socially approved warlike activities. Since this is a factor outside the sphere of sexual growth, this should extend our thinking to new lines.

Thirdly and last, it seems to me an error not to consider the details of the adolescent revolt in the light of side issues, disturbing as they may be. If we wish to maintain the developmental point of view, then it is of less significance in what manner the adolescent behaves in the house, in school, in college, or in the community at large. What is of major importance is to know which type of adolescent upheaval is best suited to leading to the most satisfactory type of adult life.

4

A Short History of Child
Analysis
(1966)

It seems realistic for psychoanalysts to begin a new venture with a historical survey since this acknowledges the part which past experience plays in present actions and in expectations for the future. For this reason I suggested to the Program Committee of this new Association that their first meeting should be opened by a look back to the beginnings of child analysis, however abbreviated such an introductory account may have to be under the circumstances.

Presented at the first scientific meeting of the American Association for Child Psychoanalysis, in Topeka, Kansas, on April 9, 1966. First published in *The Psychoanalytic Study of the Child*, 21:7-14, 1966.

THE WIDENING SCOPE OF PSYCHOANALYSIS IN THE 1920s

Child analysis as a subspecialty of psychoanalysis appeared on the scene approximately forty years ago. At the time this happened not as an isolated new departure but as part and parcel of what we call in retrospect the "widening scope of psychoanalysis." While until then analytic therapy had been confined in the main to young adults and the neuroses, from that era onward other ages as well as other categories of disturbance were included in its field of application. In Vienna, it was Siegfried Bernfeld who began with the analytic study and treatment of disturbed *adolescents*; August Aichhorn who pioneered in the field of *wayward youth*; Sadger who specialized in *perversions*; Paul Federn who experimented with the treatment of *psychotics*. In Berlin, Alexander and Staub turned to the study of *criminals*. In this extended area of work, child analysis occupied no more than a section, represented almost simultaneously by Hug-Hellmuth and after her by me in Vienna; by Berta Bornstein, Melanie Klein, Ada Mueller-Braunschweig in Berlin; by Steff Bornstein in Prague, and by Alice Balint in Budapest. Since this was before formal psychoanalytic training had come into being, none of the people named, except perhaps Hug-Hellmuth and Ada Mueller-Braunschweig, were in a teacher-pupil relationship to each other. Ideas as well as techniques developed individually and independently.

VIENNA: CHILD ANALYSIS IN SOCIETY AND INSTITUTE

It was a step forward in the line toward more systematic development when I was asked to talk on child analysis within the framework of the newly founded Vienna Institute of Psychoanalysis, a course of four lectures which appeared 1926/27 under the title of *Introduction to the Technique of Child Analysis*. As was the habit then, the course was attended by most members of the Vienna Psychoanalytic Society, and it stimulated in some of them the wish in their turn to embark on experimental work in the newly opened field. It was followed therefore by a first Seminar on Child Analysis, a regular meeting in which cases were presented, technical innovations described, and theoretical conclusions put up for discussion.

It was in this seminar that Berta and Steff Bornstein, Editha Sterba, and Jenny Waelder Hall presented the child cases which became landmarks in the literature of child analysis. Other active participants, among them some founding members of this Association, joined earlier or later, in the late '20s and early '30s, as they completed their analytic training and entered the Vienna Psychoanalytic Society. To name only some, in alphabetical order: Dorothy Burlingham, Edith Buxbaum, Erik Homburger Erikson, Hedwig and Willie Hoffer, Anny Angel Katan, Marianne Kris, Anna Maenchen, Margaret Mahler, E. Menaker; and as psychoanalytic students from abroad: Marie Briehl, Julia Deming, Edith Entenman, Margaret Fries, Elisabeth Geleerd, Margaret Gerard, Mary O'Neil Hawkins, Rosetta Hurwitz, Edith Jackson, Estelle Levy, Marian Putnam, Margaret Ribble, Helen Ross.

I consider it in line with later developments that even in these early days the new venture into the area of childhood did not remain restricted to therapy but was carried further into the fields of application and prevention by means of a Course for Educators, founded by Willie Hoffer. Here, teachers from nursery schools, elementary schools, and high schools were introduced in careful, consistent, and painstaking manner to the principles of psychoanalytic child psychology and to their relevance for the understanding, upbringing, and teaching of children of all ages. The results of this instruction are open to view in many valuable articles published in the *Zeitschrift für psychoanalytische Pädagogik* of which Willie Hoffer soon became editor. The alumni of the Vienna Course for Educators can still be found in responsible positions in the children's field all over the world, and quite especially in the United States.

TWO SCHOOLS OF CHILD ANALYSIS

It was not to the advantage of the development of child analysis that from the outset the new movement proceeded on two lines, distinct from each other. While the Vienna school of child analysis grew, on the whole connected with my name, the Berlin, later London, school developed simultaneously under the leadership of Melanie Klein. Differences which seemed to be confined at first to the area of technique spread increasingly to essential points of theory as publications followed each other.

So far as we were concerned, we explored above all the alterations in the classical technique as they seemed to us necessitated by the child's inability to use free association, by the immaturity of his ego, the dependency of his superego, and by his resultant incapacity to deal unaided with pressures from the id. We were impressed by the strength of the child's defenses and resistances and by the difficulty of interpreting transference, the impurity of which we ascribed to the use of a nonanalytic introductory period. This latter difficulty was removed later by Berta Bornstein's ingenious use of defense interpretation for creating a treatment alliance with the child patient. As regards the specific motivation for child analysis, we learned to see as our long-term aim the preventing of arrests and inhibitions, the undoing of crippling regressions and compromise formations, and, thereby, the setting free of the child's spontaneous energies directed toward the completion of progressive development.

In Melanie Klein's school of child analysis, no similar concerns about technique played a part since with them, from the outset, free play was seen as a full equivalent of free association and accepted as the basis for symbolic interpretations and as the vehicle of transference. The new theory of early development which emerged as the outcome of their findings concerned in the main the struggle between the life and death instincts at the beginning of life, the splitting of objects into good and bad, the role of projection and introjection in the building up of the personality, the overwhelming importance of orality. In fact, according to this theory, it is the events of the oral, not of the phallic-oedipal, phase from which the main features of superego and character formation as well as the roots of mental illness have to be deduced.

THE TEACHING OF CHILD ANALYSIS

If there was one point, nevertheless, on which the two schools were in full agreement, it was the form in which instruction was offered to their candidates. Obviously, at that early date, no technique of child analysis could be more than an outcrop of the classical technique for adults, i.e., a variation and adaptation of the latter, developed from it by trial and error. Accordingly, no student of psychoanalysis was supposed to embark on such experimentation before he was sufficiently rooted in the adult technique. We had seen too much of the danger of "wild analysts" in the adult field to wish to produce a similar breed for the treatment of children.

On the basis of such considerations child analysis was —and still is being—taught in the official institutes strictly as an addition to the regular training course for adult analysis. In some places, candidates are permitted to treat a child after their first adult case, in others after their second or third cases. More often than not, adult training has to be completed altogether before training in child analysis is permitted to begin.

So far as teaching is concerned, it is therefore the most significant advance in recent years that we believe to have at last developed an independent approach to the analytic therapy of the child, and that we can now instruct people in this technique as an alternative to adult analysis, i.e., before, or simultaneously, or after their supervised adult cases. Or to put it differently: it does not matter as much any more at which end of the scale we initiate child training; just as child analysis can be acquired as an addition to adult training, so can adult training come in as a second period additional to child analysis (either, of course, based in the usual way on personal analysis plus course and seminar instruction).

An independent training course in child analysis was implemented for the first time in Hampstead after the Second World War, and has produced by now sixty-seven graduates who work actively in psychoanalytic child therapy and child study in England, in the United States, and in other continents and countries. A second course, built on the same lines, has opened more recently under Anny Katan and Robert Furman in Cleveland, Ohio. A third, devised by J. P. Teuns, is on the point of being opened in Leyden, Holland, with supervisory help given by the teaching staff of the Hampstead Course and Clinic. It is a significant point that this last-named training comes into being not only tolerated or sponsored by a branch society of the International Psycho-Analytical Association, but fully integrated with the teaching program of the Dutch Society and Institute of Psychoanalysis.

With this last step taken, child analysis has made an important move toward independent existence. Candidates are not trained directly anywhere for the analytic treatment of either psychotics, perverts, delinquents or criminals, and no technique, more or less equivalent to the classical technique, is taught anywhere for use with these categories of patients, as the child analytic technique can be taught at present. It is perhaps this unique status of child analysis among the other subspecialities of psychoanalysis which has culminated in the present venture: the formation of an independent American Association for Child Psychoanalysis.

CHILD ANALYSIS AS THE GATEWAY TO APPLICATION, OBSERVATION, AND RESEARCH

Application to the Children's Services

In line with similar developments in the adult field, child analysts in their turn moved from the therapy of disturbed children to the general study of children of all kinds, and from there to the application of the knowledge gained to the problems of educational and preventive work.

The Vienna Course for Educators mentioned above, far from being or remaining the only attempt of its kind, was preceded and followed by a whole host of similar ventures in which the principles of psychoanalytic child psychology were not only taught but actually put to the test in practical work with children. There is a direct line from Kinderheim Baumgarten, founded after the First World War by Siegfried Bernfeld and Willie Hoffer, by way of the Jackson Nursery (1937-38) to the Hampstead Nurseries in the Second World War (1940-45), and from there again to the Nursery Schools of the James Putnam Clinic in Boston, Mass., of the Child Study Center at Yale, New Haven, of the Child Development Center in New York, the therapeutic Nursery School in Cleveland, The Master's Nursery in New York, the School for Nursery Years in Los Angeles, the Orthogenic School in Chicago, the High Wick Hospital for Psychotic Children in Hertfordshire, England, and the Nursery Schools for Normal and for Blind Children in the Hampstead Clinic, London. There is also the untiring work done on the basis of psychoanalysis with well baby clinics, with pediatricians and on pediatric wards, in short-stay and in long-stay hospitals, with residential institutions, foster parents, etc. Many of these tasks were, and still are, uphill ones since they are carried out in the face of opposition derived from ingrained traditional attitudes to teaching, nursing, medical or institutional routines; they are no less rewarding for this reason, of course. The indivisibility of body and mind in the first year of life, the close interaction between emotion and intellect, between object relatedness and stimulation, between the defensive and the adaptive processes were the main insights brought to bear on the problems of child care.

Direct Observation as a Source of Knowledge

Apart from the practical results achieved by means of these labors, there was considerable gain from them in the form of added knowledge as evidenced in a small number of books and a large number of articles published in *The Psychoanalytic Study of the Child* and elsewhere. Nevertheless, in spite of many insights gained into essential processes of child development, into phase-adequate conflicts and behavior problems, into the interactions between children and their object world, etc., this method of exploration remained more or less haphazard and unsystematic until Ernst Kris set up a laboratory for himself at the Yale Child Study Center (appr. 1950) and opened up the possibilities for the systematic longitudinal study of young children. This was carried further after his death by Eleanor Pavenstedt in Boston, and in Yale by Marianne Kris, Seymour L. Lustman, Sally Provence, Samuel Ritvo, Albert Solnit. We do not forget that it is due to Ernst Kris if today we automatically link up areas which were deliberately kept separate before him, such as the microscopic and the

macroscopic approach to child study; manifest surface
behavior and unconscious id content; reconstruction of the
past and prediction of the future; in short, that we owe it
to his endeavors that the observation of children outside
analysis is now accepted as a legitimate second source of
knowledge for the analyst.

Margaret Ribble, Margaret Fries, René Spitz in the
United States, John Bowlby, James Robertson in London
are notable independent contributors to the same field.

Psychoanalytic Research

In line with the developments in adult analysis, and as
Melanie Klein, D. W. Winnicott, and their followers had
done from the outset, our child analysts also extended their
interest gradually from abnormal to normal psychology.
In our case this meant the move from a theory of childhood pathology to the recognition of a hypothetical norm
in the processes of mental growth, and from there to the
construction of a developmental metapsychology. With
this new "widening of the scope," new tasks opened up for
us and new responsibilities developed.

It is a basic fact for all analysts that the same technique
serves both analytic therapy and analytic exploration. Nevertheless, the official psychoanalytic institutes, following
the tradition in which they were set up initially, train carefully in its former use and in comparison neglect the latter.
Thus, candidates are guided how to extract the maximum
information from transference, resistance, dreams, other id
derivatives, or ego mechanisms; how to time their interpretations; in short, how to cure their patients. They receive
no guidance in such important matters as how to record

their material, or sift and summarize it, or verify their findings, or pool them with others; how to trace the history of psychoanalytic concepts, to inquire into their definitions, and to clarify and unify their technical terms; how to select specific areas for their research interests or to become alerted to the gaps in our knowledge. Not that these latter activities are not pursued abundantly in the analytic community, as evidenced by the analytic journals and book publications. But they are left more or less completely to individual effort and individual ingenuity, or at best to postgraduate opportunities which exist in some localities and are lacking in others.

In fact, it was the wish to provide such missing facilities which led to the building up of the departments of the Hampstead Course and Clinic. At least so far as child analysis is concerned, the various facets of psychoanalysis are treated there as if they were on a par, and students are from the beginning of their training systematically introduced to psychoanalysis as a method of treatment; as a tool to use for exploration and study; as a theory in need of scrutiny and expansion; as a body of knowledge capable of application to a wide number of needs in the community. What is left to the individual candidate is the final selection of one or more of these part aspects of psychoanalysis for his future career.

I would like to think that this new Association, on the occasion of its first convention, is committing itself to a similar wide outlook on the subject and thereby will shape the future of child analysis in the United States so far as analytic child therapy, analytic child psychology, analytic child study, and analytic child services are concerned.

5

Some Thoughts about the Place of Psychoanalytic Theory in the Training of Psychiatrists
(1966)

Meeting with alumni of the Menninger School of Psychiatry, as I am doing on the occasion of this reunion, and comparing them to graduates of other psychiatric training centers, I am impressed by their different attitude toward psychoanalysis, a difference which has to be attributed, I believe, to the unusual circumstances of their training.

Address to the 20th Reunion of the Menninger School of Psychiatry, Topeka, Kansas, on April 2, 1966. First published in the *Bulletin of the Menninger Clinic*, 30:225-234, 1966.

PSYCHOANALYSIS IN THE MENTAL HOSPITAL

In the ordinary confines of a mental hospital, the psychiatrist-in-training at best encounters psychoanalysis as a therapeutic method. As such it is one among many, and compared with the efficiency of the organic, electrical, and drug therapies certainly not the most potent one in use with severely ill patients. Consequently, the student has no reason to develop a very favorable opinion of psychoanalysis and no chance to acquire knowledge of its further potentialities. Under such conditions, many end their period of residency with a negative impression in this respect.

PSYCHOANALYSIS AT MENNINGER'S

There is a striking contrast between this limited outlook on psychoanalysis and the opportunities offered at Menninger's where analysis is presented not only as the basis for a psychotherapeutic technique but as an essential means of understanding the vagaries and varieties of human behavior as they are on view in the many different sections of the Menninger Foundation. The Children's Division, the Adolescent Unit, the Inpatient Hospital, the Outpatient Department, the Geriatric Unit represent a vast collection of individual case material; departmental work done with outside organizations such as schools, child guidance clinics, family services, law courts extends this to provide insight into the problems current in a social community. In fact, it would need only the further addition of a maternity hospital, a well baby clinic, and a nursery school to present psychiatric residents with the full range of human problems as they arise from the cradle to the grave.

Since psychoanalytic thinking is used throughout to high-light the problems, to clarify manifest behavior, and to unravel the unconscious motive forces underlying it, the young psychiatrist is bound to acquire a lasting respect for the analytic concepts as well as some personal impression of their theoretical applicability and practical potentialities.

PSYCHOANALYSIS IN THE PSYCHOANALYTIC INSTITUTES

We may well ask why such extensive facilities for demonstration of material should be deemed necessary to give psychoanalysis a place in the training of psychiatrists, while no recognized institute of the American Psychoanalytic Association or the International Psycho-Analytical Association offers its candidates any similar opportunity to study human beings at all periods of life, under all possible circumstances, and in a variety of interactions with each other.

The answer to this question is not difficult to find. The rigorous training of psychoanalytic candidates is based not on the direct observation of gross, overt manifestations, but on the passive and active experience with the psychoanalytic technique, i.e., the use of a method which penetrates into the mental apparatus itself and yields minute pictures of its working. Whether the analytic candidate is involved in his personal analysis, or whether, concurrently and subsequently, he applies the classical analytic technique to the few patients treated by him under supervision, in either instance the method of *free association* brings him into closest contact with the *contents of the mind*; his own or his patients' *resistances* reveal the internal, i.e., intersystemic or intrasystemic, *conflicts* and struggles within the mind; his own or his patients' *transference* phenomena inevitably disclose the quality of *object relations* and the range of interpersonal relationships, past and present, as well as the *power of the past over the present*. Thus, the analytic candidate learns from the microscopic view of himself and of a very small number of patients what the psychiatric resident has to gather macroscopically, without the help of the analytic technique, from an almost unlimited range of human beings, conditions, situations, etc.

Perhaps the psychoanalytic candidate would also draw additional profit from direct observations being added to the analytic, reconstructive method which he is taught. Nevertheless, at present, in the official training schemes, the two approaches are kept strictly separate, and are beginning to merge only occasionally where analytic investigation into early childhood, especially into the preverbal period, is concerned.

THE PSYCHIATRIST'S MATERIAL: ITS VALUE FOR THE PURPOSES OF ILLUSTRATION

Where the psychiatric resident's contact with his patients proceeds without benefit of free association, outside the intimacy of the analytic setting, and without reproduction of past experience in the transference, quantity of observational opportunity has to make up for its quality, and this all the more so since any type of human material seen macroscopically cannot be expected to illustrate more than one or the other single analytic concept.

Severely ill, psychotic inpatients, being the resident's main concern in ordinary mental hospitals, offer valuable illustration of one particular area, namely, the crude fantasy content of the id. In these cases the fantasy content is visible to the naked eye since it is stripped bare of all overlay and of the working of the ego mechanisms which normally defend consciousness and reason against the id's intrusion. Observers of such material may thus become experts in the knowledge of the unconscious mind, impressed by the *power of the id over the ego,* and convinced of the easy victory of unreason over reason. On the other hand, their understanding of the infinite complexities of human nature will be hampered by the fact that what is demonstrated to them are breakdown products. To see the mental apparatus at its worst, its working interfered with, deteriorated or destroyed, does not create the atmosphere in which its almost miraculous, intricate functioning can be appreciated. There are few psychiatrists, therefore, who, solely on the basis of such experience, will become ardent psychologists, or the equivalent to it: receptive to the complications of psychoanalytic thinking.

The various *neuroses,* on the other hand, even if seen macroscopically, supply the observer with impressions of a different kind. The anxiety shifts and the evasive maneuvers of the phobic; the ingenious interplay between impulse and defense in the symptomatology of the obsessional; the cruel, self-criticizing severity of the superego in depressed and suicidal patients—these can hardly fail to illustrate the mental mechanisms functioning at full force. What impresses one here, in contrast to the psychoses, is the *power of the ego* to keep impulses in check, to control, to build up defensive barriers, to act as intermediary between the internal and external necessities, or at least, where no permanent balance is achieved in a character structure, to

remain interlocked with the other internal agencies in un-
ending struggles. It may be no exaggeration to say that it
is the prolonged contemplation of the neurotic conflicts
which creates in the observer the wish to enter the mental
battlefield in the role of therapeutic agent. When this
happens, the first step has been taken to achieve in the
psychiatrist an analytic approach to the dynamics of the
mind.

That it is contact with the neuroses and not with the
psychoses by means of which this important development
is promoted, contains a significant hint for the training of
psychoanalytic candidates proper—a hint that so far has
not been taken seriously by the official education committees. Most future analysts, under present conditions, enter
their training after several years of working only with
psychotics, and therefore often with their psychological
enthusiasm dampened and with preconceptions of the
wrong kind.

There are, of course, many concepts essential to psychoanalytic thinking which the neuroses, no less than the
psychoses, fail to illustrate overtly. The secret *pathways
between body and mind*, for example, although they become obvious in psychosomatic manifestations and hysterical symptomatology, remain invisible as such in adult
patients unless they are brought to the surface by detailed
analytic work. On the other hand, these same interactions
between soma and psyche can be demonstrated *in natura*
with many of their normal and pathological implications
if *infants in the first months* or year of life are available for
purposes of illustration. Here, every emotional upset,
whether caused by frustration, deprivation, anxiety, as well
as every change of affect in the child (or mother) can be

shown to have visible repercussions on the physical side, i.e., to upset the feeding, sleeping, elimination processes of the infant, just as every bodily disturbance, whether intestinal, bronchial, infectious, etc., can be shown to produce an anxious, or angry, or unhappy state of mind, rendering the infant prone to emotional withdrawal and regressive losses of recently acquired developmental gains. Impressions of this kind, if available to the psychiatric residents, will not easily be forgotten in the future.

The difference between the *primary and secondary thought processes*, and between functioning according to the pleasure principle or reality principle, is appreciated by analysts during the interpretation of dreams and the unraveling of fantasies. For those who are not engaged in that type of work, these theoretical concepts can become practical realities when they observe normal children in the second year of life whose behavior vacillates from moment to moment between impulse-driven wish fulfillment and sensible, reasonable action in the service of exploring and adapting to the realities of their environment.

The utter *dependence* of human beings on their *love objects*, as revealed to analysts by the transference phenomena, can be demonstrated to observers in full force via the various forms of separation distress of young children if these are seen on the *pediatric ward of a general hospital*, a residential home for the deprived, etc. The manifestations of the *oedipus and the castration complexes* are on view in any *nursery school* where sufficient scope and freedom are allowed for play and fantasy expression. The later battle for *freedom from the infantile objects* is amply exemplified by the overt revolt of *adolescents* against their parents or, under group conditions, against parent substitutes in charge.

Usually, psychiatrists experience little difficulty in believing in the infantile *stages of pregenital sexuality* since the existence of these is evidenced for them by their reemergence in the various *perversions* involving the use of the mouth, the anus, the phallus, as in fellatio, exhibitionism, sodomy, fetishism, homosexual practices, transvestitism, etc. Similarly, those psychiatric residents who attend *law courts*, where they meet the failures of social adaptation, will appreciate more readily the immense internal struggles against instinctual satisfaction and for *law abidingness* as they normally take place in the maturing human personality.

It is a matter of greater subtlety for the observer to collect the evidence for the *regressive processes*, normal and transitory, in many *childhood* phenomena; for pathological and potentially permanent, in the *neuroses, psychoses, perversions*, etc.; and for normal but permanent, in the patients on the geriatric wards.

That the observaton of *old age* has more to offer than merely a demonstration of the power of the involutionary processes has been shown convincingly in a recent article by Grete Bibring (1966) describing a psychiatric study of old age patients in the Beth Israel Hospital, Boston. While, with the decrease of genital sexuality, the impulses are seen to regress to more infantile patterns of wishes and satisfactions, the lessening of pressure from the side of the id simultaneously creates for the ego a greater sense of freedom and an increased ability to cope with reality. This, according to her, enables the onlookers to watch the gradual emergence of what is commonly called the "wisdom of old age."

FRACTIONAL KNOWLEDGE
AND ITS APPLICATION

As matters stand at present, it is unlikely that many schools of psychiatry will have at their disposal the facilities for observation which are open to the alumni at Menninger's, nor is it likely that all the residents here will avail themselves in equal measure of the whole range of opportunities which are offered to them. This inevitably restricts the extent of the psychoanalytic data to which the individual psychiatric student has access.

It needs to be remembered further that every set of phenomena on view in the departments for children, for adolescents, for the aged, for neurotics, for psychotics, etc., even if it throws into relief one isolated psychoanalytic concept, leaves other factors in obscurity, although they may be equally operative in the same situation. Therefore, information gathered from this type of observation is of necessity fractional and leaves gaps in knowledge. These gaps have to be filled before the knowledge can be applied successfully to the many human problems in the management of which the psychiatrist in our days is expected to participate.

Applying psychoanalytic insight, for example, to the *prevention of mental illness,* an endeavor which has been the concern of the mental hygiene movement over the years, it is not enough to concentrate attention on the most obviously disturbing factors such as the deprivations and frustrations inflicted on the individual by his love objects, or the upheavals, anxieties, and conflicts threatening him from within his own mind, both of which become conscious and visible in neurotic and psychotic patients.

Nevertheless, while aiming at the avoidance or abolition of these influences in prevention, the psychiatrist also needs to know that the same factors are ubiquitous in normal life, where they play a less obtrusive and less demonstrable part in helping to build up the personality. Undue optimism and resultant disillusionment in preventive work can be avoided only when insights into all areas of the mind are balanced against each other in this manner.

When the psychiatrist cooperates with the pediatricians or surgeons on a children's ward, he likewise has to complement his vivid impressions of the children's separation distress by extensive knowledge concerning the general repercussions of physical pain and illness on the child's mental state and on progression or regression in development. The latter phenomena are less dramatic and immediate, less open to view, and more subtle than the former. Nevertheless, insight into both is needed for effective consultation.

When psychiatrists act as consultants in the *school system*, they will realize that not one set but a whole array of psychoanalytic data is needed for the task of helping teachers with their problems. Displacement of curiosity, or its inhibition, from the area of infantile sexuality to the wish for, or the avoidance of, general knowledge can be applied by the psychiatrist to explain a pupil's aptitude or incapacity for learning; tolerant or repressive handling of a child's aggressive impulses at home can be shown to have its effects on a pupil's ability or inability to compete in school; sibling rivalry within the family can be used to explain rivalry with peers within the classroom.

Apart from these familiar items of knowledge, there are some further significant insights which the school psychiatrist should possess but which are ignored by many. One refers to the fact that the pupil-teacher relationships are not replicas of the child's emotional tie to either parent but are something *sui generis,* a later, more complex, and more neutralized relationship to a group-leader figure and that the interactions between them have to be understood and handled on this basis. The second insight is concerned with the fact that success in school demands more from a child than the sublimation of some infantile impulses; that there is, indeed, a whole line of development which can be traced from the young child's indulgence in play to the older child's effort at work: while play is interrupted as soon as it ceases to be pleasurable, work is sustained regardless of immediate pleasure gain until a desired end result has been attained. That these two last-mentioned points have frequently been neglected by psychiatrists or insufficiently knowledgeable analysts in their role as consultants has led to much cháos and confusion in the modern school.

In work with the *courts* as well, much of the estrangement between psychoanalysis and the law could have been avoided by a more balanced outlook on the part of expert psychiatrists. Insight into the criminal act should be based evenly on two informed views of it: on the one hand, as the personal solution of individual internal conflict; on the other hand, as the conspicuous and implicitly dangerous failure of an individual to adapt his actions to the standards of his social environment. While psychiatrists hold the former, and the court the latter outlook, hostile clashes between the two professions are at present inevitable.

METAPSYCHOLOGY AS THE LANGUAGE OF PSYCHOANALYSIS

The considerations expressed above indicate some of the restrictions and limitations to which the application of manifest analytic data is subject. Such data are useful in themselves since they supply for the psychiatrist an entry into psychoanalytic thinking. Nevertheless, that any one set of phenomena illuminates either fantasy content or ego defense, or structural conflict, does not imply that the process is reversible, and that the same set of problems can be handled successfully by applying only these particular concepts to their management. What the psychiatrist has learned so far are, as it were, the first single phrases of a foreign tongue which have to be linked up with each other, enlarged on, and built into the correct grammatical fabric of a language.

The language of psychoanalysis—if it is permissible to carry the metaphor further—is, then, the psychology, normal and abnormal, which is the product of its technique and underlies its application, i.e., the metapsychological theory. According to it, no picture of a human being, or human action, or human phenomenon in general is complete unless it is seen from a variety of aspects.

To construct, for example, the correct image of a person in accordance with metapsychological requirements, the individual is viewed, on the one hand, as a product and particle of his background and, on the other hand, at least in adulthood, as an almost closed psychological system, i.e., as a psychological structure in its own right.

As the latter, every part of the structure has to be assessed developmentally. The sexual and aggressive drives as well as the individual's object relationships have to be traced through the consecutive stages of his growth. His ego has to be scrutinized according to the status of its apparatuses, its functions, its defense organization; his superego, according to its negative and positive aspects, the object relations, and other sources from which it is derived.

Since the division of the personality is carried out according to areas or parts, each with its own manner of functioning and pursuit of its own aims, the ensuing clashes between drive fulfillment, reality adaptation, and pursuit of ideals are taken as inevitable. The particular conflicts which arise from them have to be described in detail since their form, content, and intensity determine either the individual's mental health or, under unfavorable circumstances, the type, extent, and severity of his pathology.

Conflicts are also described according to the relative strength of the psychic forces which are engaged in them, as well as according to the mental qualities of consciousness, preconsciousness, or unconsciousness attached to them.

CONCLUSION

It remains an open question whether, and by what series of steps, the psychiatrist in training will pass from the initial encounter with manifest analytic data to this type of combined genetic, dynamic, structural, quantitative, and adaptive thinking which comes naturally to analysts. There are some, undoubtedly, who will be content not to go beyond their introduction to the subject. Others may wish to increase their knowledge through constant widening of their field of observation, or through intensive study of the literature, or through both. For many, one or the other modification of analytic technique in dynamic psychotherapy will prove a useful tool for further exploration. There will also be those who remain discontent with their knowledge and frustrated in their efforts, until they have gone the whole way and learned to apply the classical psychoanalytic technique itself to themselves and others.

In any case, the more complete and integrated the analytic information which has been acquired, the more efficiently can the appropriate concepts be selected from the whole body of the theory and applied, wherever needed, to the material in the psychiatrist's field of work.

6

The Ideal Psychoanalytic
Institute: A Utopia
(1966)

The responsibility for selecting the topic for this presenta-
tion lies with Dr. Heinz Kohut, who also chose its title,
adding the qualification of "utopia" to a heading which
otherwise might have sounded controversial. Left to myself,
I should have been less careful and inclined to call this talk
"A Description of a Psychoanalytic Institute as I Think It
Ought to Be."

I am reminded in this connection of an attitude of mine
which stems from the remote past. At the age before independent reading, when children are read to or told
stories, my interest was restricted to those which "might

Presented at the Chicago Institute for Psychoanalysis on December 21, 1966. It is published here for the first time.

be true." This did not mean that they had to be true stories in the ordinary sense of the word, but that they were supposed not to contain elements which precluded their happening in reality. As soon as animals began to talk, or fairies and witches, or ghosts to appear—in short, in the face of any unrealistic or supernatural element—my attention flagged and disappeared. To my own surprise, I have not altered much in this respect. The Ideal Psychoanalytic Institute also claims my interest only insofar as it is capable of becoming true. Accordingly, there will be nothing in my description of it which excludes this possibility.

THE PREREQUISITES FOR PSYCHOANALYTIC STUDY

It is my predilection for a realistic outlook, in fact, which determines my attitude to the first task with which all our psychoanalytic training committees are faced, namely, that of deciding which academic subjects are most effective in preparing applicants for the study of psychoanalysis. There is a hint concerning this in Freud's *Question of Lay Analysis* (1926b) which is worth noting. What he said there runs as follows: "If—which may sound fantastic to-day—one had to found a college of psycho-analysis, much would have to be taught in it which is also taught by the medical faculty: alongside of depth-psychology, which would always remain the principal subject, there would be an introduction to biology, as much as possible of the science of sexual life, and familiarity with the symptomatology of psychiatry. On the other hand, analytic instruction would include branches of knowledge which are remote from medicine and which the doctor does not come across in his practice: the history of civilization, mythology, the psychology of religion and the science of literature. Unless he is well at home in these subjects, an analyst can make nothing of a large amount of his material" (p. 246). It goes without saying that it is tempting for me to pursue a plan of this kind and to enlarge on its implications. But, as matters stand at present, I have to admit to myself that it is in truth a piece of "fantastic" wishful thinking, and as such I have omitted it regretfully from the image of the Ideal Institute.

This, of course, does not imply that I have also abandoned the conviction that several branches of science and several disciplines directly concerned with human beings are profitable as avenues leading to the profession of psychoanalyst. Even if under present circumstances we are powerless to achieve as preparation for the individual candidate the appropriate combination of knowledge stemming from a variety of fields, we can at least insure that—as happens in most European institutes—an equivalent mixture is created in the student body as a whole. By admitting candidates from most of the disciplines mentioned in the above quotation, we also predetermine the character of the membership of the local society in question, as well as the future membership of the International Psycho-Analytical Association. There is no doubt in my mind that this does and will enrich, widen, and safeguard the future development of psychoanalysis in all its aspects, every individual member contributing to the field on the one hand on the basis of his analytic training, on the other hand on the basis of previous thorough immersion in an allied valuable discipline.

SELECTION PROCEDURES
IN THE IDEAL INSTITUTE

Whenever we select from a wider background, we are also confronted by a greater diversity of personalities among the applicants. As carefully as it is done at present in most of the recognized institutes, every effort will also be made in the Ideal Institute to rule out the more severe psychopathologies and character disorders such as psychopathy, psychotic risks, depressive risks, perversions, and delinquent trends. At the same time, the methods used for the purpose may differ markedly from the selection procedures used at present in some of the more ambitious and adventurous institutes. The Ideal Institute will adopt in this respect a position outlined several years ago by Heinz Kohut in a yet unpublished essay on the "Selection Process." Kohut emphasizes "the influence of the selection procedure itself upon the candidate" since this is "the first encounter of the future psychoanalyst with organized psychoanalysis." He stresses that here the future analyst forms a first image "of what analysis is like and how an analyst behaves." He contrasts "the slow and careful consideration of the defenses" in the analytic process with the "efficient selection procedures where secrets are quickly wrested from the candidate through the use of psychological tests, group interviews, stress situations or deeply probing individual interviews."[1]

It will be argued here that the analytic process as applied to patients can afford to be leisurely, while selection of candidates implies the necessity to arrive at immediate

[1] When Kohut's essay, written in 1961, came to my knowledge, I decided to take his warnings into account whenever I had to share the responsibility for selection procedures.

decisions and that, for these, facts have to be collected by whatever means; that it is not possible to combine the latter aim with the analyst's habitual respect for the individual personality, for character defenses, reservations, etc. —in short, with a truly analytic atmosphere.

There is, I believe, a valid way of countering this argument. It seems to me that for a long time we have underrated and neglected the psychoanalyst's potential abilities to draw diagnostic conclusions from the manifest picture of a personality and that, in the selectors at least, this ability should be developed until it becomes a fine art. What will be used in the Ideal Institute for the purpose is a Metapsychological Profile of each applicant. This is a schema for which the Developmental Profiles of children and adolescents and the Diagnostic Profiles of adults as they are used in our Hampstead Clinic are the prototypes. Such Profiles are constructed essentially from conclusions drawn from manifest material, i.e., surface and behavioral data which allow the experienced analytic diagnostician (or selector) to draw conclusions as to the unconscious processes and repressed contents which lie behind them. By developing the art of Profile-making, the members of the selection committee will be able to maintain their analytic reserve while simultaneously constructing an informative picture of the applicant's personality.[2]

There are some additional points, objective as well as subjective, which may serve as further guides to selectors. Objectively, it will be recommended that they pay some attention to the question whether applicants for training have made some previous spontaneous approach to ana-

[2] For the detailed description of the Developmental Profile, see *Writings*, Vol. V, chs. 3 and 4, and Vol. VI, ch. 4.

lytic literature, or whether they have left such reading to the course requirements of the future. The former attitude will be taken to signify a genuine wish and search for what analysis has to offer, the latter to betray an indifference which points to ulterior motives for choosing this particular profession. I am aware of the fact, of course, that this statement is not reversible. Not every eager reader of psychoanalytic literature is a good prospective candidate since such reading may be prompted by severe pathology, by defensive intellectualization, etc. Still, the point is made that ignorance of psychoanalysis, which is a good thing in a future patient, may have the opposite predictive value in a future candidate.

Subjectively, selectors in the Ideal Institute will be careful not to set up regulations which would have ruled out themselves in the role of applicants, whether this concerns their own professional backgrounds or their own characters and personalities. There is no reason to demand from candidates ideal qualities and perfections which the selectors themselves do not possess.

I know, further, that at present the members of more than one training institute have devised measures to check up on the efficiency of their own selections. This is done, usually, by following up the individual candidates' progress in the training, and by comparing their success or failure with the initial impression given by their personalities and the predictions made for them. Useful as this method may prove in the long run, my Ideal Institute will proceed differently in this respect. There, selectors will be asked to look not into the future of the candidates but into the past of the psychoanalytic movement. They will find that essential technical, clinical, and theoretical contributions to psychoanalysis have been made by individuals not only on the basis of different professional backgrounds but in spite of, or prompted by, all sorts of personal characteristics, qualities, and idiosyncrasies. To imagine these historical figures in the role of present applicants for training may do much to dispel prejudices and to lessen some of the restrictive practices which govern selection at present.

TIME COMMITMENT TO THE IDEAL INSTITUTE

The future Ideal Institute agrees fully with the present organizations so far as the *aims* of psychoanalytic education are concerned. High among these ranks the major experience which the candidate undergoes in his personal analysis, an experience which is also meant to give him a new outlook on life and the environment. He has to become familiar, further, with a new clinical psychopathology. He has to acquire the skill of a new and exacting psychotherapeutic technique. He has to be led beyond the understanding of the pathological to a new general psychology embodied in the metapsychological theories. For this purpose he needs to be introduced to a literature which, by now, has grown to vast proportions.

While sharing these maximum objectives with our official training institutes, the Ideal Institute parts company with them regarding the hope that they can be achieved in a comparative minimum of time.

What I have in mind here is not the duration of the analytic training as such. I am well aware that this has been extended gradually from the original few months or one to two years to last at present in some institutes three years, in others four or even five. But for all that, apart from the personal analysis and supervision, it has not become much more intensive. As it was done fifty years ago, candidates still spend their working days in nonanalytic surroundings and nonanalytic pursuits. They still arrive for their clinical and theoretical seminars and lectures in the evenings or on weekends, i.e., tired out and unreceptive, at times when, by rights, they should be at leisure and pursue their personal lives and interests within their families. They are still lectured to by senior members of the profession, who devote some off-time to teaching, often against their real inclination, and only too often without having developed any teaching skills. Candidates still have little or no time left for reading, apart from the most urgent course requirements, or for pursuing spontaneous theoretical interests. To the best of my belief, there is no other serious and ambitious discipline where part-time training schemes of this type are adopted, or where they are expected to be effective.

The argument that this is traditional, i.e., time-honored, in psychoanalysis does not seem appropriate. Our pioneering analytic institutes of the past were poor, and even to provide cases and treatment rooms for supervised analytic work stretched their resources to the utmost. Of necessity, analytic candidates had to earn their living outside of analysis. There was no money for training grants or registrar posts, or for creating a paid training staff. It may be that even now financial hardships are not absent from the candidates' lives; but even if it is so, the same is no longer true of the psychoanalytic organizations and communities as such. It is difficult to understand, therefore, why our present institutes do not establish their own residencies. This would provide them immediately with full-time students, able to pursue their psychoanalytic studies intensively, leisurely, and with enormously increased profit. The present part-time system seems as out of date to me as if church services were still conducted in catacombs since this is where the early Christians were obliged to meet.

Following these considerations, the Ideal Institute will accept only full-time candidates, will establish analytic residencies for them, and will fill their working time by means of a schedule in which the time demands for personal analysis, supervised clinical work, theoretical pursuits, independent reading, and incipient analytic research are carefully balanced against each other. Senior staff will be available, and paid, i.e., people who regard the teaching of psychoanalytic clinical and theoretical knowledge as a major job.

THE PERSONAL ANALYSIS OF CANDIDATES

If there is one area of the training where no major changes are envisaged in the Ideal Institute, it is that of the candidates' personal analyses. As stated above, great advances have been made in this respect during the last thirty or forty years. The candidate's personal analysis is regarded not only as the most essential part of his training; it is also much more thorough and extended over a much longer period of time than it used to be. Any shortening of the duration of an analytic session, any lessening of frequency of sessions during the week, is regarded with suspicion in most institutes. The benefits derived from these arrangements are unlikely to be disputed in the future. Of the various methods now in operation (whether the personal analysis should precede, or accompany, or outlast clinical training), the Ideal Institute will choose the second eventuality; namely, candidates will be expected to be under analysis for the duration of the training period, after which time the decision about termination or continuation becomes their personal concern.

There is, though, one particular insight which will have to be established before a candidate of the Ideal Institute is dismissed from his analysis, namely, that he enters a profession in which his personality will be continually at risk and that, therefore, for him the analytic process will have to be an ongoing one, interminable rather than terminable. That this may imply future returns for analytic help will not be viewed as a sign of pathology or of failure.

CLINICAL TRAINING OF THE CANDIDATE

Supervised Clinical Work

It will be left to the analyst's and analysand's joint decision how soon or late after beginning analysis and after commencement of the introductory courses, the candidate enters the institute's residency program, in which from then onward all his working time is spent. Unlike present institutes, the Ideal Institute provides equally for work with adults and with children. Since we now possess a technique of child analysis which is not merely a derivative of the adult technique, but equivalent to it, it is no longer necessary to relegate child analysis to the end of training after the candidate has familiarized himself thoroughly with the classical technique. As matters stand now, and will stand at the time when the Ideal Institute comes into being, it will depend on the previous professional background and on the personal preferences of candidates whether they enter into their clinical work on one or the other end of the age scale, beginning with the treatment of adults and ending with that of children, or vice versa. They will be trained in both and may specialize in either in the future. It goes without saying that two sets of supervisors are available for the two purposes, and that the candidate can make his choice from them.

During my own lifetime, the technique of supervision has changed from the original occasional help extended by an older to a younger colleague to the calculated fine art, as it is described, for example, in the recent book by Joan Fleming and Therese Benedek (1966). The Ideal Institute will adopt, of course, these most recent advances and exploit them to the full. Simultaneously it will also consider and weigh against each other the advantages and disadvantages of active and passive learning, of dependence versus independence, of personal style versus prescribed procedure. Not all candidates respond to technical guidance with the same readiness and there will always be some who learn best the hard way, i.e., by trial and error.

Sharing of Clinical Material

The resident's timetable in the Ideal Institute will normally allow for not more than four or five treatment cases, a number which is hardly sufficient to orient him in the clinical field. For this reason, the candidate is introduced to another pursuit which is considered vital, namely, to the sharing of clinical material with his colleagues. He is encouraged to offer the material of his own cases to the other members of the institute who, in their turn, have to throw open theirs to him.

To accomplish this interchange effectively, much has to be taught, and learned, which is not included in the syllabus of present institutes. In the Ideal Institute, candidates will not only report to their supervisors. In addition to this, they are requested to lay down their findings in weekly, three-monthly, and yearly reports, in what can be termed increasingly higher levels of abstraction. By formulating, dissecting, summarizing, and evaluating their data, and by placing them in analytically meaningful categories, they will learn to turn the undigested mass of items as they are elicited in every analysis into material which can be profitably assimilated, understood, and used by every analyst.

Once this skill has been acquired, it becomes possible to establish the clinical working groups which will be the characteristic of the Ideal Institute. There may well be groups (or workshops) of two kinds: those where the case material is taken from patients of one and the same age group, including all clinical types (child analysis, adolescent analysis, analysis of adults); and those where one clinical type is chosen for study, pursuing this particular pathology through all ages and developmental stages (hysteria, phobia, obsessional neurosis, perversions, addictions, character disorders, etc.). To make discussion in these workshops profitable, it is essential that all written material is exchanged among the participants and studied before meetings, time for this being provided as a matter of course in the curriculum.

Since no analyst in training can assimilate and retain in memory more than a very limited number of cases, in addition to his own, the number of members in each working group will be kept small.

Utilization of Clinical Impressions

Clinical training in the Ideal Institute will be expected to serve more than one purpose. Analyzing under supervision is expected to increase the candidate's receptiveness to and understanding of the derivatives of the unconscious and to develop his skill in handling transference and resistance phenomena. Pooling material from his own cases with those of his colleagues will provide increased opportunities to see the mental apparatus at work under a variety of pressures and conditions; to watch the interplay of internal with external forces; to appreciate the difference between intersystemic and intrasystemic conflicts; to understand symptomatology as attempts at conflict solution, etc. All these are invaluable clinical impressions gained at a time when the analytic novice is at the most receptive stage of his career, and more ready than later to have his eyes opened and to correct previous misconceptions. Medically qualified candidates are relieved to see the mental agencies in their comparatively undamaged state, not out of action or reduced to breakdown products as they are in the psychoses. Former academic psychologists among the candidates profit especially from observing overdetermination and multiple function in psychic life and from realizing the impossibility of isolating variables for the purpose of study as they were used to do in laboratory experiments. Candidates with a background in education are impressed by the antithesis between their past and present work, i.e., with the internalizations and permanently established regressions and compromise formation which deprive a personality of fluidity, invalidate the possibility of further development, and have to be removed by analytic work before any external approach or change can elicit suitable responses.

TRAINING IN THEORY

A major point, at present under discussion in most institutes, is the question whether psychoanalytic theory should be taught historically or according to subject matter. Convincing arguments are used on both sides. Adherents of the historical method claim that understanding of psychoanalysis is greatest where the newcomer is helped to trace the slow and laborious path of the pioneering workers; adherents of the opposite side are reluctant to spend valuable teaching time on concepts or theories which they, as well as the students, consider to be outdated.

So far as the programs for the Ideal Institute are concerned, I have found myself unable to take a decisive stand with regard to either method, and I would opt rather for a constructive compromise between them. After a short, introductory history of psychoanalysis, I believe teaching should be geared to concepts, but, there, adhere strictly to their historical development. Defense, anxiety, instinct theory, ego and superego concepts, the various metapsychological aspects, etc., all have their own historical development and can be understood only on the basis of this development. Taken singly, this introduces the student to selected chapters of psychoanalytic theory; taken in their entirety, they add up to a history of psychoanalysis as such.

There is a further reason why, to me, it does not seem urgent to decide from which particular angle psychoanalytic theory should be presented first. This question acquires major importance only where candidates act as passive recipients of knowledge in their training, i.e., where they rely altogether on systematic syllabi, prescribed reading lists, and strict sequences of information which are handed out in formal lectures. According to my plans, none of this is going to take place in the Ideal Institute. Students will be expected to enter actively into the new field and explore the unfamiliar discipline in a spirit of adventure and discovery. Theoretical courses will be no more than a method of guiding the candidate toward independent reading. Reading lists will be banned since they cannot list everything and their omissions might be misunderstood as pointers to what need not be read.

The Institute will consider itself successful only if it is able to create an atmosphere in the library where the whole of the existing literature is flung open and placed at the disposal of the future analyst. It is then up to him to select from what is offered and in this selection to be guided by points of interest arising from his personal analysis, or from his own case material, or from the cases of his colleagues. What will be considered of major importance will be that he should wish to read what he is reading, i.e., that the activity should be a cathected one. Whether in this pursuit he begins with the ego and ends up with the id will be as irrelevant as whether he begins with the present and ends up with the past, or vice versa.

There are merely minor steps from this type of active study to the first contributions which every newcomer to the field can make to its upkeep and extension. Individual students, on the basis of their own theoretical interests and predilections, can be entrusted with the task of pursuing an individual theoretical theme through the literature from its first appearance to the present day, accompanying the theme with their own critical remarks and speculations. What is too difficult for the individual can be entrusted to a group (a theoretical workshop), which can be formed on the basis of joint interests, where controversies can be fought out and lively discussions can arise and be enjoyed. Where advice and assistance from a teacher are desired, it will be available, of course. For this type of work, too, time will be provided in the students' daytime schedules.

Carried through in this manner, theoretical training in the Ideal Institute will cease to be the chore which it represents now to many overburdened candidates. Naturally, long-distance stimulation in the place of set lectures demands a better class of teachers, but so far as the future institute is an ideal one, it is expected to produce these in time.

INTRODUCTION TO DIAGNOSTIC EVALUATION

The syllabus of the Ideal Institute will include a further item, in this case one of which analytic training so far has fought shy: namely, diagnostic evaluation.

From the past, we have brought with us the idea that diagnosis of the patient's disturbance at the first contacts with him is not a truly analytic concern. After all, a diagnostic assessment at the beginning of treatment can be little more than a collection of snap judgments. The deeper material, i.e., the id contents, the repressed matter, the unconscious parts of ego and superego, the interactions between them which go on under the surface of the mind— all are elicited only during treatment and are not available for assembly at its beginning. Analytic students have been taught over the years to wait patiently until, at a later stage or after termination of treatment, reconstructions can be carried out and the structure of the patient's personality can be presented.

In earlier days, I myself supported this point of view which I now oppose as no longer justified. In the last twenty or thirty years we have learned much about the links between depth and surface and have grown more knowledgeable in using communicated conscious material, behavioral items, surface data of all kinds, and manifest symptomatology for deducing from them the internal processes and unconscious contents which underlie them.[3] This enables us to construct approximate pictures of the patients' personalities at almost any point of contact with them, i.e., diagnostically, during treatment and after termination of analysis. Spaces which are left blank in the picture in the beginning are filled in gradually during the analysis and shadowy or tentative outlines become more firmly defined as the analysis proceeds.

It goes without saying that such assessments are not communicated to the patients, nor do they promote interpretations or shorten treatments. They are useful in a different way, namely, as the basis for critical discussion in a diagnostic study group; as an exercise in thinking in which the theoretical and clinical approaches are brought to bear jointly on the same material; as a starting point for prognostic predictions which will be checked at later dates against the results of the analysis.

Where such pictures of patients are set up at the beginning and end of analytic treatment, candidates can also be introduced to the important pursuit of evaluation of

[3] For a new approach to the classification of childhood disorders on the basis of manifest symptomatology, see ch. 10 in this volume.

treatment results. Where merely symptomatic gains have been achieved by the patient, this will show in the meta-psychological picture as shifts in the area and mode of conflict solution. Where truly analytic changes have been brought about, they will be evidenced by significant changes in the cathexis of fixation points, undoing of id and ego regressions, abandonment of primitive defense mechanisms for those of a higher and more complex order, etc.

INTRODUCTION TO DIRECT OBSERVATION

Diagnostic work of the type described above will also introduce candidates to the idea that the observations of an analyst are not necessarily restricted to the analytic setting. Even though the latter is uniquely devised to lower ego controls, to encourage regression, to ease upsurges from the id, and to engineer the return of the repressed via the transference, there are also other situations in life where similar exposures take place spontaneously and where either contents of the mental apparatus or samples of its working are in view of the observer.

In the Ideal Institute, candidates will be encouraged toward the end of their training to check what they have reconstructed in the consulting room against the open displays of psychic material as they are available in the various institutions of the community. Undistorted id contents, freely demonstrated by severe psychotics on the psychiatric wards, are well known, of course, to the medically qualified, and should be made available to all other candidates at this stage. Reconstructions in analysis of the first year of life and of the early mother-infant relationship will be checked against observations in maternity hospitals or in young families. Psychosomatic phenomena are nowhere more in evidence than in the daily routine work of the infant welfare clinics. The all-important transition from primary to secondary process functioning and the fluctuations between the two modes are exemplified almost step by step in the behavior of young children in a nursery school. The same is true for their "regression rate" and the beginning sublimations.[4]

There will be no danger that concepts such as those of the libidinal stages and their substructures will remain artifacts in the minds of future analysts if reconstruction of the past in analysis is supplemented by the same analysts actually witnessing these developmental processes at the time of life and in the life situations where they occur. Also, failures of social adaptation and breakdowns of super-ego functioning become vivid when illustrated by visits to the courts, by discussion with probation officers and other personnel, etc.

PRACTICAL AND THEORETICAL APPLICATIONS OF PSYCHOANALYSIS

When the Ideal Institute sends out candidates for direct observation of meaningful behavior, it will be on guard against a possible misunderstanding of purpose which, at present, spoils the success of such ventures in some of the few institutes where they are undertaken. The candidates will go to maternity wards, welfare clinics, nursery schools, juvenile courts, etc., strictly as observers, by no means as

[4] As Ernst Kris (1951, 1955) has shown.

advisors; their visits will have a learning, not a teaching function. To become a consultant in one of these applied fields is a further step, and one which cannot be undertaken lightly.

It is one of the unsolved problems which I foresee for the future of the Ideal Institute that even after four years of full-time work when personal analysis, clinical and theoretical training are far advanced, there will be reluctance to dismiss students as qualified. What has not yet been learned, or taught, are the applications of psychoanalysis without which no analytic training is complete.

There are two main ways of applying psychoanalysis to the allied fields. One is by varying the classical technique to fit other purposes, as in adult psychotherapy, in child psychiatry or in parent guidance. The other consists of utilizing the theoretical knowledge and insights gained in psychoanalysis for the problems of upbringing, of teaching, of general medicine, of pediatrics, of the law, of the prevention of bodily and mental illness. To confuse the two modes of application, for example, by bringing analytic techniques into the schools in place of analytic understanding, is a grave mistake, often made, which has frequently brought psychoanalysis into disrepute.

To date, applied psychoanalysis has not been included in the syllabus of present psychoanalytic institutes. Modified analytic techniques for psychotherapy with adults and children are taught in many places by many analysts. This teaching is also left to many nonanalysts, which is not to its advantage.

As regards the application of analytic insight to the various disciplines named, this is not taught at all at present. Here the Ideal Institute will have to devise its own teaching methods and will have to contend with the difficult fact that an effective analytic consultant to any of them needs to be familiar with both fields, a capacity which is not easy to achieve except on the basis of the candidate's preanalytic professional background.

Finally, what is left are the applications of psychoanalytic knowledge to the humanities, i.e., to literature, history, sociology, religion, etc. Hopefully, the candidates of the Ideal Institute will acquaint themselves with these in the course of their wide reading.

CONCLUSION

I trust that I have kept my promise and that there is nothing in this blueprint of the Ideal Institute which will prevent the utopia of today from becoming a reality of tomorrow. The only serious problem which will have to be met is the financial one. Here I am confident in the idea that money is usually found for worthwhile purposes; and that the training of true analysts, equally versed in human understanding, clinical insight, therapeutic skill, and searching exploration, ranks high among these.

7

Acting Out
(1968 [1967])

ANALYTIC CONCEPTS AND THEIR FATE

When the Program Committee of the Copenhagen Congress selected "Acting Out" as the subject for its main Symposium, it joined the ranks of those who are concerned with the history of psychoanalytic concepts in general and interested in tracing the vicissitudes of their individual fates in detail. Varied as these fates are, it is not impossible to single out some distinctive trends and pursue them through the theoretical, clinical, and technical literature.[1]

Opening paper on the main theme of the 25th International Psycho-Analytical Congress, Copenhagen, presented on July 24, 1967. First published in the *International Journal of Psycho-Analysis*, 49:165-170, 1968.
[1] See in this respect also the work of the Clinical and Theoretical Concept Groups of the Hampstead Child-Therapy Clinic, under the chairmanship of H. Nagera.

There are some terms and concepts without which psychoanalysis could not have done in its beginnings since they served to convey meaning in a simple manner to a public otherwise unprepared for the new findings. An example of this was the idea of *complexes*, an expression used to designate any cluster of drive derivatives, thought representations, and affects rooted in the unconscious, and from there giving rise to anxiety, defensive maneuvers, character distortions, and symptom formations. This was a convenient way of describing, as it were, in psychological shorthand, whatever people suffered from as a father complex, mother complex, guilt complex, inferiority complex, etc. Eventually, the very umbrella nature of the term militated against its usefulness, and with increasing knowledge it was split up into a number of more precise notions, such as dependency (of the infant on the mother); internal conflict (between the agencies of the mind); severity of the superego (guilt feelings); depression; penis envy; etc. The term complex was retained exclusively for the vitally important experiences centered around the triangular relationships in the phallic phase (oedipus complex) and the anxieties concerning the loss of the male sex organ (castration complex).

Other analytic concepts took a turn in the opposite direction: starting out as precise, well-defined descriptions of specific psychic events, they proceeded from there to indiscriminate application until they ceased to be meaningful. Appropriate examples of this are the concepts of *transference* on the one hand and *trauma* on the other hand. Transference (and countertransference) originally meant the distortion of a realistic patient-analyst relationship by additions from past unconscious and repressed object relations; this notion was widened until it comprised whatever happens between the two partners in the analytic setting, regardless of its precipitating cause, derivation, and meaning. Trauma, in its turn, went all the way from its original use for damage to the stimulus barrier caused by excessive excitation to the designation of any experience with pathogenic potentiality (retrospective trauma, cumulative trauma, silent trauma, "beneficial" trauma, etc.), until, recently, strenuous efforts were made to reinvest it with its original significance (see Furst, 1967; see also ch. 14 in Writings, Volume V).

There is a third development, more relevant still to our present purpose than the two preceding ones. Most psychoanalytic concepts owe their origin to a particular era of analytic theory, or to a particular field of clinical application, or to a particular stage of technical procedure. Only too frequently they are then carried forward unaltered from this point, regardless of changes in these fields. Notwithstanding their having been firmly rooted in their home ground, they cease to fit the changed circumstances, where they lead an uneasy existence and lend themselves to all kinds of theoretical misconceptions. It seems to me that the concept of "acting out" belongs in this category, and it is my hope that the present Symposium will make some contribution toward clarifying the confusion.

THE CONCEPT OF "ACTING OUT" DEFINED IN ITS ORIGINAL SETTING

The term "acting out" (*agieren*) made its first appearance in 1914 in Freud's essay on "Remembering, Repeating and

Working-Through."[2] There "acting out" is defined, in contradistinction to remembering, as the compelling urge to repeat the forgotten past, and to do so within the analytic setting by actually reliving repressed emotional experiences transferred onto the analyst and "also on to all the other aspects of the current situation." Such acting out was understood to replace the ability or willingness to remember whenever the patient was in resistance. "The greater the resistance, the more extensively will acting out (repetition) replace remembering" (p. 151).

This apparently simple statement in the setting of "Further Recommendations on the Technique of Psycho-Analysis" nevertheless needs to be understood within the wider framework of the classical theory of the neuroses, of which it forms a part, as well as within the theory of psychoanalytic therapy, which is dependent on it. The relevant points of these theories can be summarized as follows:

(i) that neurotic symptoms are the result of compromises between repressed drive derivatives and the repressing forces which oppose them;

(ii) that the dynamic struggle which underlies neurotic symptoms is not an event of the past but a present-day force, i.e., that there are constant upsurges from the side of the drive derivatives which have to be held in place by an equally constant countercathexis from the ego agencies;

(iii) that the analytic technique aims deliberately at upsetting this balance, which is precarious in any event, and that it succeeds in doing so, on the one hand by the introduction of free association which sets aside controls,

[2] Actually, the term "acting out" was used earlier by Freud, e.g., in the postscript to the Dora case (1905a [1901]). I have been reminded of this fact by Dr. Daniel Prager.

weakens defenses, and encourages irruptions from the id; and on the other hand by providing in the person of the analyst a present-day object onto whom past emotional experiences can be transferred;

(iv) that struggles between analyst and patient ensue due to the fact that in the analyst's intention this reliving of the past is meant to increase remembering, while from the aspect of the patient's id it has one purpose only: to attain belated satisfaction for formerly frustrated strivings and to do so via the appropriate actions.

The foregoing explains why the correct analysis of any neurotic patient has to be expected to be a stormy procedure with uncertain results. In fact, the possible outcomes of the battle between analyst and patient are of various kinds:

The analyst may be successful in depriving the id impulses of their intended satisfaction. This happens if he perceives and identifies the drive derivative at the moment of emergence in free association or in the context of a dream; or if he deflects it from its path by means of interpretation and thereby causes its discharge into thought and verbalization. Where this occurs, the relevant drive derivative, until then part of the forgotten past and as such subjected to primary process functioning, enters into the conscious ego and is included in the latter's synthetic function. This is one way in which "id can be turned into ego."

On the other hand, not all repressed psychic content is capable of emerging in the states of widened consciousness as promoted by free association or available in dreams. The "forgotten past" may be unobtainable except in the form of being relived. If this is the case, the analyst provides for its token satisfaction in the transference. The result is a repetition of the past in behavior, but one on which the analytic rules are imposed. The patient's acting out toward the analyst is restricted to the re-experiencing of impulses and affects, the re-establishing of infantile demands and attitudes; but it is supposed to stop short of motor action and to leave the basic treatment alliance between patient and analyst intact (attendance at sessions, punctuality, obedience to analytic rules such as honesty, free association, etc.). Acting out in the transference within these limitations was already in the early days of psychoanalysis recognized as an indispensable addition to remembering. On the one hand it safeguarded the continuance of analytic work in the face of resistance; on the other hand it opened the door for the re-emergence of material from deeper layers of the personality. Resistance and (acting out in the) transference thus became the mainstays of the analytic technique. As before, the analyst's aim remained to recognize and grasp hold of the revivals of the past as they emerged, now in behavior, to interpret them, and to incorporate the regained id material within the confines of the ego.

There always remained the third possibility which meant a defeat to the analyst's effort. The power of the "forgotten past" or, rather, the strength of the repressed strivings may militate against any form of reduced relief or token gratification, and sweep beyond the imposed limits into motor action. In the transference, this may break the treatment alliance and put an untimely stop to the analysis. But acting out of this kind by no means restricts itself to the analytic situation. The patient, who directs his impulses into the motor sphere, also relives what emerges from the unconscious in his ordinary life, and may harm himself by

it. Or, even where the harm is negligible and only tempo-
rary, such impulses, once discharged and thereby deprived
of their emotional cathexis, do not lend themselves in the
same way to effective analytic interpretation.

So much for the classical view on acting out. To sum it
up once more: acting out is at a minimum, i.e., nipped in
the bud, so far as the technical devices of free association
and dream interpretation are concerned. It is allowed lati-
tude, within the limits of the analytic rules, in the transference and for the sake of transference interpretation. And
it endangers the progress of analytic treatment when it
cannot be confined either within the psychic sphere (short
of motor action) or within the analytic setting (i.e., within
the transference).

THE CONCEPT OF "ACTING OUT" IN A CHANGING THEORETICAL SCENE

In the historical phase described above, the proportion between recovery of the past via free association and dream
interpretation (i.e., remembering) and recovery of the past
via transference behavior (i.e., reliving, repeating, acting
out) was a fairly even one, with the latter regularly taking
precedence over the former merely in periods of resistance.
This technical balance was altered decisively, following
certain later changes in theoretical outlook.

Foremost among these was the shift of analytic interest
and exploration from the phallic-oedipal events (as the
precipitating cause of neurotic conflict) to the preoedipal
ones and notably to the early mother-infant interactions
with their oral implications and repercussions on the rudiments of personality development. This "forgotten past,"

especially so far as it refers to the preverbal period, has never entered the ego organization in the strict sense of the term; i.e., it is under primary, not secondary repression, and therefore is not recoverable in memory, only apt to be relived (repeated, acted out, in behavior).

Another relevant shift was the analysts' extension of interest from the id to the ego. This was already foreshadowed in 1914 when Freud described that the patient does not *remember* his defiant or critical attitudes toward his parents but instead revives them toward the analyst; that he does not remember having been ashamed of his infantile sexuality but instead is ashamed of being in analytic treatment, etc. The more ground the ego and its mode of operation gained in the analytic process, the more heavily the analyst relied on the transference of infantile attitudes (i.e., on repetition, acting out) to provide the material for interpretation.

Even the widening of the instinct theory to include aggression had similar technical consequences. The sexual urge proliferates in conscious and unconscious fantasy and can be interpreted on the basis of night dreams, daydreams, and the images produced in free association. In contrast, the aggressive drive is more closely linked with action and the motor apparatus, i.e., more liable to be acted out than to be remembered.

Increasing concentration on the preoedipal phases, psychoanalytic ego psychology, and the changes in instinct theory thus are responsible for almost all the innovations which characterize the present-day technical outlook of most analysts. There is a growing disbelief—not shared by everybody—in the therapeutic effectiveness of remembering.[3] As a logical consequence of this, we find in many quarters a decreasing interest in free association and dream interpretation (as the "royal road to the unconscious") and an increasing insistence on reliving emotional experience and repeating it (acting it out) in the transference. Since new attitudes rarely avoid the extreme, we also find that many analysts now tend to neglect important material if it does not find its way into transference behavior; or that they make frantic endeavors in interpretation to change all emerging images, thoughts, and memories into transference material, regardless of whether this happens or does not happen spontaneously in the patient's mind.

Wherever the technical rights and wrongs of this may lie in detail will be decided in time by the successes or failures of psychoanalytic interventions. What is in evidence at present is, without doubt, a swing in the technical balance toward greater reliance on reliving (i.e., acting out) in the transference, and with it also an increased tolerance for those extreme forms of acting out which by-pass the analytic situation, invade the patient's external life, and can only secondarily be drawn back and interpreted in the transference.

THE CONCEPT OF "ACTING OUT" IN THE WIDENING SCOPE OF PSYCHOANALYSIS

In using the term "acting out," it should be remembered how closely the original concept in its technical sense was wedded to the circumstances of the adult neurotic for whom it was first coined, i.e., to the idea of a personality

[3] See James Strachey (1934) on "mutative interpretation."

with sufficient ego strength to enforce neurotic compromises on the drives; with secondary process thinking and the synthetic function of the ego fairly intact; with the ego in control of motility; and with sufficient maturity to replace action by thoughts and words under the ordinary conditions of waking life. According to this definition, such individuals were considered to "act out" when they were put under pressure by the analytic technique, i.e., when their controls were diminished deliberately, the warded-off id content tempted to rise to the surface, and the inhibitions or symptomatic manifestations swept aside sufficiently to permit the "forgotten past" to express itself in action.

When analytic therapy moved from its original field of application to the transference neuroses to include other diagnostic categories as well as other age groups, the circumstances were no longer the same. Nevertheless, the concept, or rather the term, of "acting out" continued to be used.

"Acting Out" of the Impulsive Patient

A good example of this are the impulsive and delinquent character disorders, the prepsychotic, psychotic, and especially paranoid states, the alcoholics and other addicts who are now considered amenable to psychoanalytic therapy. We find in the literature that most analysts who treat them refer to such cases as "acting-out patients" and therefore discuss the technical difficulties encountered in their treatment, or the technical parameters necessary for them, under the same heading as the handling of the transference behavior of their neurotic patients. This usage of the term seems unwarranted to me. By employing the same word, the analyst fails to pay attention to changes in the meaning of the concept; moreover, the differences between the neurotic and the delinquent or psychotic type of analysand are thereby obscured instead of highlighted.

Unlike the neurotic, the delinquent, the addict, and the psychotic act out habitually; i.e., they also do so without the releasing benefits of the analytic technique. With them, the upsurges from the id, which cause their impulsive behavior, have to be understood as belonging to their pathology and not to a curative process. If one wishes to apply the term to them at all, it has to be defined anew, this time not as repeating in contradistinction to remembering, as with the neurotic, but as id-controlled action in contradistinction to the ego-controlled actions of the normal individual. We have to disregard the misleading factor that under the influence of analysis neurotic patients behave as if they were impulsive characters. It remains a mistake to reverse the statement and regard the analytic behavior of the impulsive types as on a par with the neurotic ones.

There are several important respects in which the impulsive behavior of the nosological types named above differs from "acting out" proper. One is the *quantitative* aspect: since, in their case, release of action is due not to the careful and gradual progress of interpretation but to the constant imbalance inherent in the internal structure, the dosage with all its further implications is not under the analyst's control. Another difference concerns the *direction* of the process: instead of originating within the analytic situation and affecting the environment only secondarily, the impulsive behavior of these types begins in the external world from where it has to be dislodged and drawn into the transference. The analysis of the delinquent, according to Aichhorn (1925), starts when he steals from the analyst instead of from strangers. Likewise, the analysis of the addict is initiated by his transferring his dependence on the drug or alcohol to an equivalent dependence on the actual availability of the person of the analyst.

Even where this succeeds, there is little chance of restricting the transferred strivings to the psychic sphere and to exclude their motor expressions. This is understandable since the origins of the disturbances inevitably go back to periods of life before thinking had become an acceptable substitute for motor action. Contrary to his technical expectations in the therapy of the neuroses, the analyst may have to resign himself to the fact that in these new clinical fields motor action within the treatment is not an exception but the rule. There is no doubt, of course, that in this extended form of acting out the patient also repeats his past and that memory can be extracted from the re-enactment. Whether the ensuing reconstructions serve the recovery of the patient will depend in the last resort not on the quantity or quality of the acting out itself but on the intactness or defectiveness of the ego's synthetic function to which the regained material is submitted.

"Acting Out" in Child Analysis

With the move from the therapy of adults to child analysis, the concept of "acting out" loses even more of its meaning. It is true, of course, that neurotic latency children, no different from adults, become more inclined under analysis to act on impulse; equally, that impulsive latency children do so as part of their pathology and that this habitual behavior needs to be drawn into the transference before it becomes useful therapeutically. But the younger the patients, the more do these differences become blurred and the nearer do we come to a state of affairs to which the later distinctions between remembering, repeating, reliving, acting out, etc., do not apply.

Young children who never cooperate with free association and rarely with dream interpretation are exempt from the widening of consciousness which promotes remembering. They have no organized recall for past experience and are not expected to acquire it under the impact of the analytic technique. Severe obsessional development excepted, they are unable to keep impulses within the psychic sphere; on the contrary, not thought or speech but motor actions are their legitimate media of expression and communication. Whatever impulses and emotions are aroused in treatment immediately spill over into their daily life, etc.

These age-adequate characteristics automatically classify all children before the latency period as "acting-out" patients, with the reservation that in their case the phenomenon is developmentally determined and does not carry the same significance as it does in later life, neither for highlighting alternating states of treatment alliance and resistance to treatment nor for the quality and historical level of the material which is produced.

If we want to view the technique of child analysis from the aspect of "acting out" at all, we can only define it as one where the patient is conceded the right of free motility in the session; to bring his material in the form of actions; to express his transference feelings in active behavior; to react actively to the analyst's interpretations; and, again, to work through them by means of modified activity.

The analyst, instead of striving to contain the patient's expressions in the psychic sphere and within the analytic realm, has to be content with reducing reality actions to play activity and to find his way from there via fantasy elaboration to verbalization and secondary process thinking. His final aim remains the same as in adult therapy: to submit all psychic content to the synthetic function of the patient's ego, regardless of the manner in which it has appeared (acted out with the original objects, acted out in the transference, in reality behavior, in role play, in play with toys, in fantasy etc.).

"Acting Out" in the Analysis of Adolescents

That the majority of adolescents are acting-out patients is well known. Here, again, the phenomenon is age-adequate, since at this stage recall of the past is at a minimum and reliving of past experience at its height, although the latter is modified and distorted by developmental forces.

That the adolescent is apt to act out violently within the transference is in conformity with this heightened tendency toward re-enactment. That he carries his actions beyond the confines of the analytic situation reflects his developmental need to seek experience outside the family sphere. That he is often on the point of breaking treatment is his legitimate way of reliving the urgent need to break his family ties.

Whether the adolescent's dramatized form of acting out can be turned into analytically useful material depends above all on two conditions: on the analyst's side on his skill in differentiating between past and present, i.e., between transferred and new material and between pathological and developmentally adequate elements; on the patient's side above all on the economic aspect, i.e., on the degree of cathexis of the reawakened and of the newly arrived strivings and the relative strength of the anxieties and defenses mobilized against them. Either of the latter may be sufficient to paralyze whatever ego functions need to be allied to the therapeutic task.

CONCLUSIONS

In the course of time, transference interpretation established itself increasingly as an indispensable means of technique; reliving in the transference was increasingly taken for granted; and the longer this happened, the more often was the term "acting out" not applied to the repetition in the transference at all, but reserved for the re-enactment of the past outside of the analysis. Personally, I regret this change of usage since on the one hand it obscures the initially sharp distinction between remembering and repeating and on the other hand glosses over the differences between the various forms of "acting out." To my mind, there is merit in preserving the distinctions between the consecutive steps which in this respect form a sequence in the analysand's behavior.

Memory, when widened due to free association and dream interpretation, allows the recovery of repressed fantasies and repressed, originally verbalized events. *Re-experiencing* brings back infantile ego attitudes, reproduced as regressive, dependent, or defiant feelings toward the analyst. *Re-enactment* in the transference is the means to reach preverbal experience, often by means of transgressing analytic rules. So-called delusional *transference phenom-*

ena, which for the patient have the full impact of reality and defy interpretation, are caused by very early emotional experiences, or very early fantasies, of excessive strength. Likewise, excessive quantitative cathexis of the revived strivings is responsible for the *irruptions* from the id which land the patient in repetitive *reality actions* of a psychopathic nature.

There seems to me to exist a firm link between the qualitative and quantitative properties of the "forgotten past" and the ways and means by which it is revived in analysis, whether this revival takes the form of mere remembering or happens in the guise of re-experiencing, re-living, re-enacting, or any other variety of controlled or uncontrolled repetition.

8

Indications and Contraindications for Child Analysis
(1968)

In a paper on "Indications for Child Analysis," written in 1945, I made the attempt "to find indications for the therapeutic use of child analysis not so much in the neurotic manifestations themselves as in the bearing of these manifestations on the maturation processes within the individual child."[1] Thereby I shifted the emphasis from the purely clinical and pathological features of a case to its de-

This paper was presented at the third annual scientific meeting of the American Association for Child Psychoanalysis, New Haven, Conn., on April 21, 1968. First published in *The Psychoanalytic Study of the Child*, 23:37-46, 1968.
[1] See *Writings*, Vol. IV, p. 37.

velopmental aspects, with the clear intention to let the latter be decisive for either the recommendation for or the recommendation against analysis. It seems to me the proper time to re-examine this precept, after more than twenty years of its use in private as well as in clinic practice.

THE INFANTILE NEUROSES

We have all learned to recognize as obstacles to personality growth of an individual child the *conflicts* raging between the different agencies of his internal structure, i.e., processes which consume the energy at the disposal of the person instead of leaving it available for the various tasks of life; unsuitable *defenses* against drive activity which cripple the efficiency of the ego and restrict its sphere of influence; *anxieties* which at their height create an inner atmosphere unfavorable for the smooth unfolding of important ego functions; *fixations* of large quantities of libido on early developmental stages which impoverish further psychosexual advance; *regressive moves* in the area of either drives or ego which undo development; severe *repression of aggression* which limits any kind of productive activity.

We have also learned to classify all these manifestations as internal ones. Rooted in the child's previous history, they exert their influence over his present and future life and prevent any inner equilibrium as thoroughly as they prevent adaptation to the demands of external reality. What they represent for us in their combination with each other is the essence of the infantile neurosis, i.e., the pathological state which has shown itself as eminently amenable to analytic therapy. It is in cases of this kind that we have no hesitation to declare that treatment by child analysis is clearly indicated. Only a therapy devised to reach into the extreme depth of the psychic apparatus and to revive experiences of the remote past can be expected to alter the quality of the defenses, to undo regressions, and, generally, to alter the balance of forces within the structure of the personality.

DEVELOPMENTAL PROBLEMS AND DISTURBANCES

Our recommendations for analytic treatment become much more hesitant when we are confronted with cases of another kind which, though showing some resemblance to the first-named category, differ from it in important respects. Similar to the infantile neuroses, their pathology is based on conflicts which are lodged internally; dissimilar to them, these conflicts do not exert their influence from the past but are acute and ongoing, i.e., caused by the pressures of the developmental phase through which the child is passing at the time. Children with such developmental disorders may seem affected as severely as those who suffer from a circumscribed neurosis. They are usually brought for diagnosis at the peak of the phase, i.e., at the time when their suffering is most intense.

We might arrive more easily at a decision for analytic treatment in these instances if we were not mindful of the lessons learned from corresponding clinical pictures in the life of adults. As it is expressed most forcibly in "Analysis Terminable and Interminable" (1937): "the work of analysis proceeds best if the patient's pathogenic experiences belong to the past, so that his ego can stand at a distance from them. In states of acute crisis analysis is to all intents and purposes unusable. The ego's whole interest is taken up by the painful reality and it withholds itself from analysis, which is attempting to go below the surface and uncover the influences of the past" (p. 232).

As analysts of adults we have learned to respect such reservations. Taught by repeated failures, most of us now hesitate to take patients into treatment while they are engaged in ongoing and exciting love affairs, precarious and upsetting as their course may be; or immediately after major frustrations before the individual's own ego has found time to absorb their impact; or after object loss by death during the period of acute mourning; or before impending examinations, great as the fear of them may be; or when the individual is confronted by acute physical threats such as blindness or cancer and has to come to terms with the danger of disablement or death.

As analysts of children we have to admit that most of the developmental problems of childhood closely resemble these adult situations of crisis. The oedipus complex itself is, after all, the prototype of an upsetting love affair, complete with hopes, expectations, jealousies, rivalries, and inevitable frustrations. What a young child goes through at the birth of a sibling is essentially not very different from experiences of bereavement in later life since it is felt as loss of the mother or, at least, loss of faith in the mother's love. The heightened ambivalence of the anal-sadistic phase, coupled with the projections of aggression, threatens the child with the destruction of his love objects as well as with injury and destruction at the hands of the love objects. The increase of castration anxiety which occurs normally with the onset of the phallic phase is experienced by many boys as a threat of permanent disablement. Finally, the process of development itself has the character of an exciting venture which, to speak with Greenson (1967), "may drain a patient's motivation [for analysis] or deplete his energies" (p. 55).

Faced with the necessity to decide for or against treatment of these cases, the child analyst finds himself torn between conflicting opinions. On the one hand, he knows that such difficulties are ubiquitous, inevitable, and, in fact, part of life itself. Since they are phase-bound, they are by definition potentially transitory and, with any luck, will be outgrown when further maturational advances intervene. Meanwhile it is a legitimate task for the child's ego to deal with them and the legitimate duty of the parents to support the child in his endeavors.

On the other hand, this is not the whole story. There is also sufficient analytic evidence to show that a child's ego may adopt unsuitable solutions and that these may remain permanent throughout life. Moreover, not all parents support their children in sensible endeavors. Many mishandle their offspring during these critical periods and deal more than clumsily with whatever oral, anal, phallic or aggressive problems succeed each other and complicate their lives.

It is for these reasons that many analytic observers are convinced that during the whole period of development many children are in danger and that, where actual crises develop, only analytic help, applied without delay, will be effective in avoiding crippling solutions and thereby serve a truly preventive aim.

In the diagnostic conferences of our Clinic a recommendation for or against treatment of such cases is not arrived at without all the positive and negative possibilities being aired in all directions. The decision arrived at after lengthy discussion is most often not unanimous. Usually a minority opinion advocates waiting and watching for the ego's spontaneous compromises, while the majority verdict recommends immediate analytic treatment to avoid lasting harm being done to the child's further chance of normal growth.

ENVIRONMENTAL INTERFERENCES WITH DEVELOPMENT

Difficult as the aforementioned decisions for and against analysis are, they dwindle to nothing when we compare them with the quandary of the child analyst who is faced with the multitude of children who are, quite obviously, victims of the external circumstances of their lives. It may be a confusing factor for their assessment that, in their case as well, damage is also located in their structure. But, in contrast to Group I and Group II, damage is not self-inflicted as a result of internal strife, but is caused and maintained by active, ongoing influences lodged in the environment. These influences can be of two kinds: either negative in the sense that they disregard and therefore frustrate important developmental needs of the child; or negative in the sense that they directly and forcefully act in opposition to the normal direction of development itself. In both instances the child victim is in need of therapeutic help. But in neither case is the type of help clearly indicated, nor the therapist's role in the process clearly circumscribed.

Frustration of Developmental Needs and Its Consequences

Under normal family conditions a young child's developmental needs are provided for almost automatically by the "expectable environment" (Hartmann, 1939). It is only when the environment fails the child and his needs are disregarded that the whole complex interaction between requirement and fulfillment reveals itself in detail.

That every single aspect of the child's personality is affected adversely unless definite sources of supply and support are made available to him has been proved beyond doubt by analytic work carried out with the children of severely disturbed parents, concentration camp and institutional children, orphaned children, handicapped children, etc. Not only does every infant have definite needs stemming from his unformed and unstructured state, but these needs also change and vary with ongoing development. At every stage of his growth the child needs help from definite environmental attitudes and suffers harm if this help is not forthcoming.

To remind ourselves of a few examples only:

The sufficiency of primary narcissism, and consequently the individual's later self-esteem, seems to depend on the mother's undisturbed emotional attachment to her small infant.

Pleasure in motor activity as well as later grace of movement seem to be based on the fulfillment of the infant's need to be touched and cuddled, i.e., on the satisfaction of his skin erotism. Here the mother has to play an active part in libidinizing the various parts of the child's body.

Object relationships do not mature into object constancy unless the child's first loved figures remain stable.

Archaic fears are not overcome unless the mother fulfills her role as the child's auxiliary ego.

The cognitive functions of the child's ego do not mature unless appropriate stimulation is offered at the appropriate periods. Unstimulated or understimulated children appear as mentally retarded.

Excessive defense activity leading to inhibition of function is avoided only where the environment shows tolerance toward the child's drive activity.

The ego's supremacy over the id requires as a precondition the right measure of parental guidance toward impulse control.

A boy's phallic strivings need the mother's pride and pleasure in his masculinity as their counterpart. Similarly, a girl's turn to femininity may be stopped unless it is met by her father's interested oedipal response.

Work with the blind has provided us with valuable proof how the absence of a single channel of communication between the child and his environment not only affects the development of his object relationships, and consequently his identifications, but how damage spreads from the libidinal area to the ego functions until, in the last resort, one unfulfilled need (for visual contact and stimulation) distorts the entire process of development.

In clinical practice, the referral of such cases seems to outnumber those of the two first-named groups. A more exact appraisal of the proportion between them is complicated by the fact that these multiple developmental faults[2] represent a fertile breeding ground for neurotic problems which proliferate on it to the extent that in the final diagnosis the latter more or less obscure the former. It is a further complicating factor that, regarding these disorders, the parents are much more motivated to seek therapy than they are in other instances. They may remain completely oblivious of or indifferent to a child's suffering from internal conflicts about his death wishes, his aggression, his masturbation fantasies; of his anxieties, phobic withdrawals, inhibitions or compulsions. But they become vocal and insistent in their demands for a cure if the child's immature object relations make him difficult to live with; if his intellectual backwardness affects his school performance; or if his lack of impulse control brings him into conflict with the law.

From the aspect of indication or contraindication for child analysis, basic developmental defects pose considerable problems. Therapeutic help, in answer to the parents' or the school's request, can hardly be refused since the difficulties caused by the child's abnormality are of an urgent nature. Nevertheless, once embarked on therapy, the child analyst feels doubtful of his aim and competence. He is face to face with the so far unanswered question whether and how far the neglect of developmental needs can be undone by treatment.

True to his analytic training, the therapist's efforts will be directed toward reviving the original harmful events. Since these have determined the direction and distortions of development, he will find that their impact cannot be eliminated and that his successes are confirmed to alleviat-

[2] See M. Balint (1958) on "basic faults."

ing the child's responses to their aftereffects. This means that he may have to be content to deal analytically with the neurotic superstructure which does not cause, merely overlays, the basic damage to the personality.

Therapists who are not willing to restrict themselves to this limited field may find two other avenues of approach, neither of them truly analytic. They may turn the treatment situation itself into an improved version of the child's initial environment and within this framework aim at the belated fulfillment of the neglected developmental needs. As a form of "corrective emotional" (i.e., developmental) "experience" this may be successful, especially with the very young when the original frustration of needs and their later fulfillment are not too far apart in time.

Or, as a form of family psychiatry, therapists may feel that their main work lies with the parents rather than with the child and that developmental harm, whether past or present, is undone best by the very people who have caused it initially. In this instance, therapeutic success or failure depends on three factors: on the extent to which the attitudes and personalities of the parents are normal enough to be open to change; on the extent to which the originally environmental factors have been internalized by the child and have become influences working from within; and on the unknown extent to which major developmental trends prove to be irreversible once they have been established.

For the therapeutic concerns of the child analyst it is vital to distinguish in his assessments between the neurotic and developmental disorders, in which the child's ego plays the central pathogenic role, and the "deficiency illnesses," i.e., the pathological distortions which can be traced back to the lack of some external agent that is an essential requirement for normal growth. By relieving pressure on the immature ego and by improving its spontaneous solutions, child analysis has therapeutic possibilities which are almost unlimited in the former cases. In contrast, with the latter, therapy works merely on the fringes, while underneath the child's stunted personality remains unchanged. At the worst, the benefit is not on the side of the patient at all but on that of the analyst, who from the treatment of such cases gains valuable insights into the conditions of growth and thereby acquires new weapons for carrying on the fight for safeguarding the best interests of children and, in general, for the prevention of mental illness.

Environmental Obstacles to Development

Our difficulties increase further with another category of cases in which the environmental or parental obstacles to development meet head on with some of the major internal complexes, impulses, anxieties, and fantasies of the child and intensify or fixate the latter beyond any chance of their being outgrown, overcome, or brought under ego control in the normal manner. Examples of this kind are also numerous.

We know, for instance, that there is an early phase in life, before the boundaries between self and object world are established, when the infant in his own feeling "merges" with the mother and to all intents and purposes lives in symbiotic unity with her. Normally, this phase is followed by the child's wish to establish his personal independence and identity, i.e., by the "separation-individuation phase."[3]

[3] According to Margaret Mahler (1963).

But we may well ask ourselves how separation and the establishment of a separate identity can be expected to take place in a child for whom merging is not only his but the mother's admitted need; i.e., when the latter declares openly that she feels at one with her by then five-year-old son, as if they were both an "amorphous mass" (as happened in one of our Clinic cases).

In the analysis of adults as well as children it is one of our tasks to disentangle the real personality of the parents from the projections and fantastic additions with which their image is overlaid in the child's mind so that they are turned into frightening and threatening figures. This may make us forget that not all the threats which emanate from the parental figures are products of the child's fantasy. From our clinical experience, we can quote a number of cases where a mother actually dreads to be left alone with the child since she feels compelling urges to throw the child out of the window, down the staircase, or to put poison in his food.

The wish to see the parents' naked bodies is, as we know, an integral part of infantile sexuality and, if not too severely checked, one that develops easily into the sublimated derivatives of wishing to know, to investigate, to explore the unknown. Nevertheless, its fate is different in cases where the child's sexual curiosity coincides with open exhibitionistic tendencies on the part of the parents. We have had dealings with a mother who gave way to the urge to display her genital parts to her growing boys; with a father who had to be warned off taking his small daughter to the lavatory to have her watch him urinate and at times hold his penis. Other parents are prompted by the same urge to allow their children to be present in the parental bedroom as witnesses to the parents' sex play.[4]

According to the common infantile sexual theories, parental intercourse is understood as an act of violent aggression with potential harm inflicted on either one or on both parents; impregnation, as the result of oral intake; birth, as anal output, etc. Normally, these theories change to correspond with ongoing phase development until, finally, the true facts are established and accepted by the adolescent on the basis of his maturing genitality. This advance does not happen where the pregenital meaning of the events is reinforced by the parents' actual fights or by openly displayed perverse behavior. Similarly, it is extremely unlikely that a child will outgrow his or her oedipal fantasies in situations where father or mother, either consciously or unconsciously, elevate the child to a substitute sexual partner or commit real acts of seduction with him.[5]

Where the parents themselves are innocent of such interference with development, fate may do the damage in their stead. Handicapped children such as the blind, the physically deformed, those mutilated by operations do not have the same chance as the physically normal ones to overcome their castration complex. Children who are orphaned early in life have greater difficulty than others in dealing with their death wishes which they believe to be all-powerful.[6]

[4] Dr. J. Rosen, a member of the Hampstead Child-Therapy Clinic, is at present studying our records and preparing a detailed investigation listing the effects of such parental complicity with the child's scoptophilia.

[5] See the case of a little girl, treated and described for the Hampstead Clinic by M. Mason.

[6] As an example of a physically handicapped child, see J. Novick's analytic study of a boy with clubfoot, a patient of the Hampstead Clinic.

Individuals whose childhood proceeds under the influ-ences of such experiences have a much reduced chance of growing up normally. The appeal for help, which is implicit in their precarious circumstances, is too strong to be dismissed lightly and often brings them into treatment.[7] But this does not by any means imply that child analysis is indicated for them as the treatment of choice and that its technical tools are found to be potent enough to counteract the ongoing upsetting influences. As I have said before, child analysis is most clearly indicated where the patient's fears, fights, crises, and conflicts are the product of his inner world and can be solved or dissolved into nothing by tracing their roots into the unconscious, by enlightenment, insight, and interpretation. Where the threat, the attacker or the seducer are real people, the therapeutic situation changes altogether. It is only understandable that the chances of successful therapy are reduced most in cases where the pathogenic influences are embodied in the parents themselves, i.e., in the very people who are expected to safeguard the child's mental health, and whenever this is endangered, to help him regain it.

[7] In fact, many cases of this kind are being analyzed at present in the Hampstead Clinic.

9

Difficulties in the
Path of Psychoanalysis:
A Confrontation of Past
with Present Viewpoints
(1969 [1968])

LEARNING FROM NEGATIVE EXPERIENCE

Psychoanalysis came into being as a medical psychology, in answer to the lack of adequate therapeutic measures for the treatment of neurotic illnesses. It is this unquestioned historical circumstance which obscures another, much more

Delivered as the 18th Freud Anniversary Lecture of the New York Psychoanalytic Institute, New York, on April 16, 1968. First published in the *Freud Anniversary Lecture Series*, The New York Psychoanalytic Institute, by International Universities Press, New York.

significant connection between psychopathology and the basic findings of the new discipline. What is referred to here is the fact that none of the latter could have been established while dealing with normal, healthy individuals, in whom the deeper layers of the mind remain securely hidden behind a smooth and often impenetrable surface. Only where functioning is disturbed, does this surface break open sufficiently to allow for glimpses into the depth.

In the *New Introductory Lectures on Psycho-Analysis* (1933), Freud stressed that "we are familiar with the notion that pathology, by making things larger and coarser, can draw our attention to normal conditions which would otherwise have escaped us." He compared *psychotic* patients to crystals which, when broken up, reveal their structure by the manner in which they come apart. These patients, having "turned away from external reality, . . . know more about internal, psychical reality and can reveal a number of things to us that would otherwise be inaccessible to us" (p. 58f.).

Our observations of *neurotic* patients are no less productive of information. The more seriously an individual is torn by conflicts and contradictory forces within himself, the more opportunity he provides for profitable exploration. So long as the defenses set up by a person's ego are intact, the analytic observer is faced by a blank; as soon as they break down, for example, when repression fails and unconscious material returns from the repressed, a mass of information about inner processes becomes available. Likewise, so long as secondary process thinking is maintained undisturbed, the observer's knowledge is restricted to the limited area of the patient's conscious ego; only a return to primary process functioning, as it occurs in dreams, in symptom formation, etc., opens up what in psychoanalysis has been called the "royal road to the unconscious." It is also well known that the regressions which occur in all mental disorders were, and are, the most reliable source of information regarding forward development. So long as an adult individual maintains his sex life on the genital level, the preliminary stages which have led up to it remain obscure; the pregenital organizations, consisting of his oral and anal trends, become visible only in the breakdown products of his sex life, i.e., in his perverse tendencies, his warded-off or indulged-in infantile fantasies, etc. Similarly, the regressions in ego functioning which accompany or follow the libidinal regressions provide many useful pointers to the sequences of ego growth and the gradual building up of the most vital ego functions.

On the basis of such impressions analysts developed a belief in the profitable nature of negative experience and extended this from their dealings with individual patients to their dealings with the public in general. In both instances it seemed that more could be learned from the difficulties, obstacles, and setbacks than from the triumphs, successes, and advances, to whatever degree they were achieved.

Freud himself set the trend by dealing at three different junctures with the significance of such adverse and seemingly frustrating experiences. The papers in question are "A Difficulty in the Path of Psycho-Analysis" (1917), from which the present lecture borrows its title; "The Resistances to Psycho-Analysis" (1925); and, finally, "Analysis Terminable and Interminable" (1937). While the two first-named papers enumerate and detail the obstacles met by psychoanalysis and its representatives in the world outside, the last one deals with the forces which militate against success in analytic treatments and, to some extent also, with some of the difficulties which arise within the analysts themselves.

THE PUBLIC

Freud's early papers are not reread often enough by the present generation of analysts to impress them vividly with all the advantages which they enjoy in contrast to their predecessors. A qualified analyst today, especially in the United States, will take it more or less for granted that respect is paid to his intensive training; that this will be an asset when he competes for professional appointments; that he will have no difficulty in building up a practice and earning his living; and that, if he sets out to write, he will encounter no difficulty in finding publishers or editors ready to accept his scientific contributions.

Justified expectations of this kind have to be contrasted with the disbelief, the ridicule, the suspicions, and the professional ostracism to which the first generation of analysts was exposed. They were, in fact, pioneers, not only because they ventured out into the unknown, where they had to break new ground, but also in the sense that their endeavors ran counter to and ignored the conventional restrictions of their time, that they risked their social and professional status, and, last but not least, in many instances gave up a secure and profitable career for financial uncertainties and hardships.

According to Freud's papers, these difficulties in the path of and resistance to psychoanalysis were due to its main findings and principal tenets. Those named by him were the discovery of a *dynamic unconscious*, which destroyed the myth of a "free will" and reduced the position of man to "not being master of his own mind"; the importance attributed to the *instinctual forces*, i.e., sex and aggression, in the adult and their preliminary stages in infantile life; the attention paid to psychic phenomena such as *dreams and parapraxes*, which until then had not been considered as deserving serious scientific exploration.

It is interesting and salutary to consider the evanescent nature of objections of this kind and to realize that prejudices which loom large enough in one period to create hardship and to obstruct progress can be pushed aside only half a century later as outdated and insignificant. All the evidence shows that this has happened here.

So far as the theory of the *unconscious* is concerned, of course, it may be maintained that this is still considered alien and unacceptable in some quarters. The Law (with some notable exceptions) still clings to the notion of a "reasonable man," whose actions are wholly controlled by conscious knowledge, a fiction around which the debates concerning responsibility are centered. Academic psychology (again with exceptions) adheres to methods of rigorous evaluating, investigating, surveying, and quantifying, which are aimed at the conscious part of the mind, not at the contributions to it from the unconscious.

But, on the whole, such isolated refusals of acceptance highlight rather than detract from what has happened elsewhere. It cannot be denied that for the general public the idea of unconscious motivation of behavior has become almost a commonplace; that contemporary writers have embraced it wholeheartedly; that it has exerted a powerful influence on educational methods and attitudes and changed them almost beyond recognition; that it has altered society's attitude toward mental illness, narrowed the gap between normality and pathology, and showed neurotic, psychosomatic, and delinquent disorders to be part of the common hazards of everybody's life.

This reversal of attitudes is still more conspicuous where the theory of *sex* is concerned. Contrasted with the outspokenness of the Kinsey report (1948), or, for example, the work of William Masters and Virginia Johnson on *Human Sexual Response* (1966), Freud's *Three Contributions to the Theory of Sexuality* (1905b) as well as his and other analysts' early papers on the role of sexuality, on sexual aberrations, etc., seem, if anything, discreet and diffident. No comparable storm of indignation has been aroused by the contemporary investigations; and even active experimentation is at present condoned freely as a scientific requirement, whereas mere verbal discussion was condemned in the past as an intolerable affront to the conventions.

Similarly, the myth of the *"innocence of childhood"* has disappeared from the scene without leaving much trace. Parents, educators, and the general public have become willing to have their eyes opened to the available evidence and to accept children for what they are: immature psychic structures, dominated by their emotions, by the search for pleasurable experience, and by the strength of their sexual and aggressive drives.

So far as the theory of *aggression* is concerned, two World Wars and the events of the Hitler regime have underlined and confirmed the psychoanalytic assertion that the aggressive and destructive forces are part of human nature and belong to the basic equipment of the human mind.

Even *dreams* have changed their status from being abstruse and therefore negligible occurrences to that of legitimate phenomena and worthy objects of scientific study and experiment, as the contemporary investigations on "dream deprivation" show.[1]

Taken altogether, no one who believes in an unconscious mind, who explores sex and aggression in adults and children, or who investigates dreams will nowadays be classed as an individual given to mystic leanings, or as an eccentric, or as unduly revolutionary, or even as outstandingly progressive.

Whether and how much the analysts have gained by these changes remains an open question. It is only too well known that new and unexpected difficulties often arise as fast as the familiar ones disappear. In fact, psychoanalysis finds itself today in a changing scene in which new challenges are encountered; these come mainly from three sides.

The most serious of these challenges arises in the area of therapy. At the time when Josef Breuer embarked on the "talking cure" with Anna O., there were no competitors; nor were there any when in due course talking under hypnosis was exchanged for free association. As often as analytic treatments were under fire for being too slow, too laborious, too time-consuming and expensive, patients and their families could always be sure that there was no alternative, at least not if the then current cold-water treatments, rest cures, and faradizations had already been tried

[1] See in this respect the publications by Dement (1960), Kales et al. (1964), Ernest Hartmann (1967), and from the analytic side Charles Fisher (1965).

and failed. This, as we know, has changed drastically and by now the therapies available for mental disorders are almost as numerous as those for physical ailments. Organic treatments such as fever therapy, electric shock, brain surgery for the most severe psychoses, the chemical thera-pits for depression, elation, and the anxieties exist in the field side by side with the many forms of dynamic psycho-therapy which are the direct offsprings of analytic thinking. If the latter offer short-cuts to health, family psychiatry and community psychiatry aim at making available to society as a whole facilities for regaining or maintaining mental health, which, in classical analysis, remain reserved for the individual.

Under these changed conditions it is not easy for analytic therapy proper to maintain its status and prestige. Analysts have to admit that where quantitatively massive upheavals of the personality are concerned, such as in the psychoses, the purely psychological methods by themselves are in-adequate and the organic and chemical means have the advantage over them. They do not concede the same for the neuroses. In competition with the psychotherapies they are justified to maintain that what they have to offer is unique, i.e., thoroughgoing personality changes as com-pared with more superficial symptomatic cures. Unfortun-ately, the former is not always aspired to by the patients, who aim above all at immediate relief from suffering.

In this struggle to maintain their own standards, analysts are apt to forget that they also hold another card which is not matched by any of the other treatments. Especially the psychotherapies can apply to the individual patient only what is already known about his particular disturbance, lim-ited as such knowledge still is in our times. It is only the psychoanalytic method itself which offers patient and therapist the opportunity to explore further, to add to the existing information, and thereby to increase the individual's chances to find the way to his own cure.

The second new challenge which analysts have to meet is closely connected with the altered status of analysis in the scientific world. So long as psychoanalysis was shunned and looked down on by other disciplines, it was not difficult for its representatives to remain wholly identified with their own field and proudly conscious of their own achievements. There was no occasion to feel, or act, otherwise. This changed when acceptance, or part acceptance, by the outside world opened up the possibility for cooperation, with psychiatry, medicine, education, academic psychology, the social sciences, the law, etc. The advance was welcome, of course, insofar as it realized the hopes and ambitions of the founder of psychoanalysis to have psychoanalysis grow beyond the therapeutic area and see its findings applied to the whole field of human concerns. But it also became a hazard since it lured many analysts away from their own base and created the temptation of being no longer an outsider, of becoming "recognized."

The danger inherent in this attitude is obvious, especially when analysts aspire to the distinction of being on a par with academic psychologists and to realize this ambition not merely by extending their explorations from abnormal to normal functioning but by adopting the academic methods of research, which prove unsuitable for their specific material. It is not unusual to find that analysts nowadays feel more eager to achieve standing and prestige in an allied field than in their own; or that they begin to deplore, secretly or openly, the essentially "unscientific" nature of their discipline, which does not allow for laboratory work, for confirmation of findings by experiment and control groups, and, above all, which employs the mind of the explorer as its only scientific instrument, a tool which in the eyes of the critics sadly lacks in objectivity.

For many analysts in this situation, it is not easy to keep the right balance between an overstrict isolationism, which leaves psychoanalysis stranded, and an overeager collaboration, which threatens the analyst's own professional and scientific image and ideals.

The third new challenge to psychoanalysis is of a completely different nature. It concerns the changes in the appeal that analysis has for the various sections of the population and its consequences for recruitment.

When we scrutinize the personalities who, by self-selection, became the first generation of psychoanalysts, we are left in no doubt about their characteristics. They were the unconventional ones, the doubters, those who were dissatisfied with the limitations imposed on knowledge; also among them were the odd ones, the dreamers, and those who knew neurotic suffering from their own experience. This type of intake has altered decisively since psychoanalytic training has become institutionalized, and appeals in this stricter form to a different type of personality. Moreover, self-selection has given way to the careful scrutiny of applicants, resulting in the exclusion of the mentally endangered, the eccentrics, the self-made, those with excessive flights of imagination, and favoring the acceptance of the sober, well-prepared ones, who are hardworking enough to wish to better their professional efficiency.

Apart from recruitment itself, there are other changes in the scene. Many people feel that psychoanalysis is in danger of losing the allegiance of the young, which was very pronounced at one time, especially after the First World War and in the early '20s of the century when Siegfried Bernfeld propounded the revelations of psychoanalysis to large audiences drawn from the Youth Movement. The young then avidly received and eagerly, often secretly, discussed them as the embodiment of the spirit of change, the contempt for the conventions, freedom of thought about sex and, in the minds of many, the eagerly looked-for prospect of release from sexual restrictions.

This has changed, because the young of today feel that psychoanalysis is now in the hands of the parent generation and as such suspect. For many of them it has lost the aspect of being dangerous, a forbidden matter, accessible only to the courageous, a useful weapon with which to attack society; instead, psychoanalysis is looked on and avoided as a procedure devised to deprive them of originality and revolutionary spirit and induce them to adapt and conform to existing conditions, which is the last aim they have in mind.

There is still another and more important dimension to this wholesale or partial disillusionment of the young with psychoanalysis. After all, analysis never offered anything except enlightenment about the inner world, about man's struggle within himself, about his being his own worst enemy. This conflicts with the present battle cry of youth of "man against society." But, perhaps, it has always been true that it is easier and more congenial for the adolescents to lash out against external restrictions than to struggle for internal balance. This latter fight for freedom may be acceptable to them only when it simultaneously serves the purpose of offending the real or alleged susceptibilities of the older generation.

To scrutinize and learn from the obstacles which divide psychoanalysis from the world at large does not imply the opinion that analysts should spend time and effort to improve these relations. On the contrary, experience has shown that such attempts are, at best, ineffective and, at worst, disastrous. No amount of enthusiasm, or of eloquence, or of proselytizing spirit will convince those who hold different opinions. Any analyst who goes too far out of his way to change the world in this respect may end up with meeting the demands of the world by changing the analytic theory or therapeutic procedure.

THE PATIENTS

Difficulties as Seen in 1937 by Freud in "Analysis Terminable and Interminable"

According to James Strachey (1964), Freud "was always well aware of the barriers to success in analysis and was always ready to investigate them" (p. 212). Not that this readiness was an asset so far as the reputation of analysis was concerned. Whenever the possibility of failure in analytic treatment was referred to by anybody, all analysts were accused of therapeutic nihilism, or at least of lack of therapeutic interest and ambition. Whenever Freud, or others, delineated carefully the scope of analytic efficiency, they laid themselves open to the reproach that they themselves did not believe in their own efforts. Nevertheless, the tradition to pay attention to and to learn from negative experience maintained itself intact and the obstacles to analytic therapy which are encountered in the individual patient remained the legitimate focus of the analyst's attention.

When Freud wrote, "Instead of an enquiry how a cure by analysis comes about, . . . the question should be asked of what are the obstacles that stand in the way of such a cure" (p. 221), he did not do so with the patients' common "resistances" in mind. These resistances stem on the one hand from the ego's attempt to maintain the *status quo* of defense, on the other hand from the id's stubborn clinging to distorted forms of satisfaction. Such counterforces are inevitable in every analytic treatment, are dealt with and dissolved within the analytic process, and, far from being obstacles, prove to be, when interpreted, next to the transference the best and most fruitful material on the way to analytic cures.

It was not these, but other, more subtle, and less obvious interferences Freud had in mind when he embarked on their exploration in "Analysis Terminable and Interminable."

Looking for the factors "which are prejudicial to the effectiveness of analysis and make its duration interminable," his first choice were the *quantitative* ones which determine the libido economy within a given individual and are decisive for his inner equilibrium, i.e., for the balance or imbalance in the defensive struggle between id and ego. Any excessive strength of instinct, whether constitutionally given or due to developmental reinforcement (puberty, menopause), may make it more difficult or may make it impossible for analysis to achieve its main task, i.e., to "tame" the instincts. Any weakening of the ego, "whether through illness or exhaustion, or from some similar cause," may have the same effect (p. 226).

Next in Freud's enumeration came the *qualitative* factors such as the alterations in the ego—whether "original, innate," or "acquired during the defensive struggle of the earliest years" (p. 240)—which, for example, determine the individual's selection from the possible mechanisms of defense and may restrict his advances from the primitive to the more sophisticated ones. Named here were also other characteristics such as a "special adhesiveness of the libido"; or an "excessive mobility" of it; or, as a characteristic difficult to localize in the mental apparatus, a "depletion of the plasticity," an amount of "psychical inertia," which makes the personality even of young patients "fixed and rigid" and prevents them from benefiting from the possibilities for change that are opened up by analytic therapy (p. 242f.).

To these obstacles to success in analysis Freud added others, "which may spring from different and deeper roots." Foremost among these he named the not infrequent and, by the analyst, dreaded *negative therapeutic reaction,* which had frequently been alluded to in earlier publications. He was well aware of the fact that patients during analytic treatment experience not only improvements but also exacerbations of their symptomatology, and this for a variety of reasons. He pointed to the inevitable risk of reducing the defenses of the patient who then has to meet formerly warded-off distressing id material without the relief afforded to him by the use of denial or repression; or to the obstinacy of patients (such as the Wolf Man) who increase the intensity of their symptoms even after interpretation before they can concede to the analyst the victory of having dissolved them; or to those patients who cannot permit themselves to be successful in any endeavor (including the therapeutic one) since for them success as such has acquired the symbolic meaning of fulfillment of a prohibited infantile wish.

Nevertheless, after discussing them, Freud dismissed these difficulties as less important and, in the majority, amenable to interpretation, and turned to other "negative" reactions which he considered more formidable. These are attributable to guilt, conscious or unconscious, to the need for punishment, and to moral masochism, all of which find their satisfaction in the very fact of neurotic suffering and defy the analyst's efforts to deprive them of this gratification.[2] The severe difficulties encountered in the analysis of such patients, Freud referred to as "the intervention of an element of free aggressiveness," i.e., a quantity of aggressive and destructive energy which the individual has withdrawn from use against the external world and turned inward. In this internalized form, it increases the tendency to internal conflict "irrespective of the quantity of libido" (p. 244). The result is a change in the instinctual climate itself, i.e., an ominous alteration from the search for pleasure as a governing principle to the preference for unpleasure. The latter then dominates mental functioning in the form of masochism.

In addition to this "negative therapeutic reaction," Freud also named as responsible for "interminable" analyses two factors which are rooted in the bisexual nature of human individuals. Men dread and ward off persistently their own feminine leanings toward other males, and the

[2] See in this respect Freud (1923, pp. 49-51; 1924; 1930).

resultant "rebellious overcompensation" may prove victorious over all analytic efforts. Above all, it produces an almost impenetrable transference resistance toward an analyst of the same sex and militates against the acceptance of a cure from him. Similarly, female patients, on the basis of their inherent masculine tendencies, may cling stubbornly to their wish for a penis and, instead of being cured by the treatment, may become severely depressed when they realize that the analysis can do nothing to fulfill this fantasy.

In an informative Editor's Note to Freud's expositions, James Strachey (1964) summarized that "The paper as a whole gives an impression of pessimism in regard to the therapeutic efficacy of psycho-analysis." He attributed this pessimism to the circumstance that the obstacles alluded to "are of a physiological and biological nature" and "thus in the main unsusceptible to psychological influences," as, for example, the "relative 'constitutional' strength of the instincts"; "the relative weakness of the ego owing to physiological causes"; the death instinct as being "actually the ultimate cause of conflict in the mind" (p. 211f.).

On the other hand, he also saw some more hopeful signs in Freud's remarks concerning a therapeutic alteration of the patient's ego. While earlier papers had stressed that, to achieve success in an analytic cure, the ego has to be capable of being strengthened, of being made "more independent of the super-ego," of being "widened" concerning its field of perception, "enlarged" in its organization, able to "appropriate fresh portions of the id" (Freud, 1933, p. 80), it was indicated here for the first time how such alterations could be effected. Due to the recent advances in Freud's analysis of the ego, such therapeutic changes were now seen "as the undoing of alterations already present as results of the defensive process" (p. 213).

Strachey did not stress the fact that, with Freud, a negative note crept into this subject as well. Freud was convinced that not every patient's ego lends itself to improvements of this kind. For these to come about, the ego has to be basically a normal one and "a normal ego . . . is . . . an ideal fiction. . . . Every normal [person's] ego approximates to that of the psychotic in some part or other and to a greater or lesser extent" (p. 235).[3] Thus, on this ground, too, pessimism remained and the impression was left that there are impasses which limit the extent of analytic cures and confront the analyst with problems for which no satisfactory solution was at hand, at least not at the time.

Developments since 1937

It is well worth our while to inquire what has happened in this particular field in the intervening thirty years; whether additions have been made to Freud's enumeration of difficulties; what remedies have been suggested; and where the latter has happened, whether the solutions found are technically and theoretically tenable and satisfactory.

---

[3] Freud's statements in this respect have been fully confirmed since by Charles Brenner (1968), who singles out "Archaic Features in Ego Functioning" and stresses that the very ego capacity on which the analytic technique relies most heavily, i.e., the *synthetic function,* is the one which is most often found wanting; that even so-called normal people may be able to accommodate in their functioning far-reaching inconsistencies and contradictions without feeling the need to confront them with each other, to reach compromises between them, or to embark on any other of the possible ways of their integration within the area of the conscious ego.

ADDITIONS TO THE LIST OF DIFFICULTIES

What I mention in this respect are personal impressions of my own collected in the field of child analysis. While dealing with children analytically, it has struck me that certain factors can be recognized as being significant for the success or failure of analytic therapy. Other pathological circumstances being equal, children seem to me less able to respond favorably if one or more or all of the following four characteristics are present in them:

1. A *low threshold of tolerance for the frustration of instinctual wishes.* Where this is present, any postponement or reduction of gratification becomes particularly intolerable. The quantities of unpleasure released by frustration are greater than normal and there is increased pressure toward immediate discharge of tension; this militates against the gradual modification and "taming" of instincts, which is named by Freud as the major aim of analytic therapy.

2. A *low threshold of tolerance for anxiety.* This manifests itself adversely in two ways. First, the less anxiety an individual can tolerate, the quicker he has to resort to defensive activity and symptom formation, i.e., the worse are his chances of maintaining or regaining his mental equilibrium. Secondly, he is badly equipped for meeting the quantities of anxiety which are released by the analytic process itself (through undoing defenses) and for making constructive use of them. Where anxiety tolerance is too low, interpretation of unconscious contents induces panic instead of bringing relief.

3. A *low sublimation potential.* Where the ability to accept substitute gratification is not intact or where the

person has not developed beyond primitive, crude, material needs, there are few pathways for displaced discharge and consequently it becomes more difficult to "tame" the instincts. Analytic therapy can liberate sublimations which are blocked by inhibitions and defenses; it is another, so far unanswered question whether it can also increase the sublimation potential and thereby improve the patient's chance to profit from analysis.

4. *Preponderance of regressive over progressive tendencies.* Psychoanalytic therapy applied to children counts heavily on the intactness of the wish to "move forward and complete development" (Edward Bibring, 1936). Where this is deficient, or outweighed by regressive forces, analysis is used by the child, not to resolve developmental arrests, but as a license to return to earliest levels of id satisfaction and ego expression, i.e., to effect regressions which are not in the "service of the ego" and may defy the analyst's effort to use them in the service of the analytic treatment.[4]

SUGGESTED REMEDIES

The suggestions for improvement of analytic efficiency which have sprung up in the analytic world at large can be divided roughly into two categories, each of which has a link with Freud's own remarks. They take their starting point on the one hand from the "therapeutic alteration of the ego" demanded by him, on the other hand from the notion that the ego distortions which hinder analysis are

[4] For a more detailed discussion of these four points, see *Writings*, Vol. VI, ch. 4.

acquired by the individual during his *earliest* defensive struggle against unpleasure.

As regards the need for a *therapeutic normalization of the ego* during the analytic process, and for the benefit of it, this was immediately taken up and acted on by many of Freud's co-workers and pupils. To quote only a few among many, past and present: that it is one of the aims of analysis to change the relations of the ego to id and super-ego (Edward Bibring, 1937); that in analysis the ego is induced to stop or alter defenses and to tolerate id derivatives which are less and less distorted (Otto Fenichel, 1937); that the analytic technique is devised, point by point, to fit the capabilities of a normal ego and that technical parameters become necessary to match deviations from the norm until these are corrected therapeutically (K. R. Eissler, 1953); that the ego has to be made more tolerant (Strachey, 1934, 1937); that the intrapsychic modifications brought about by analysis have to include the ego (Gill, 1954); that "permanent changes" have to be effected in the ego, "thereby extending [its] power and sovereignty" (Greenson, 1958).

Actually, this increased emphasis on the analysis of the ego (sometimes referred to as "defense analysis") brought with it no major changes of analytic technique. It served merely to stress points which had been made before, but had not always been implemented seriously enough: that, during the analytic process, defense has to be interpreted before the id content which is warded off by it; that to approach id contents without that precaution amounts to "wild" analysis; that the analyst's attention has to be divided equally between content and defense and continually turn from one to the other; that regression in the transference brings with it not only the fantasies and anxieties of infantile life but also the modes of functioning and expression which were characteristic of the past; i.e., that it enlightens analyst and patient not only with regard to past emotional experience but also with regard to past ego functioning, including its deficiencies.

The increased attention paid to the ego during the therapeutic process brought to an end the period when analysis was alluded to exclusively as a depth psychology and turned it into "analysis of the total personality" in the true sense of the term. There is no doubt that this improvement of technique helped the analyst in many cases and was the factor that made it possible to include "character analysis" in the scope of analytic therapy.

The analysis of the ego for therapeutic purposes was linked, further, with Heinz Hartmann's studies of the ego, which began in the early '30s of this century. Heinz Hartmann oriented his investigations toward the origin of the ego, the development of its psychological apparatuses, its energy problems, its adaptive function, i.e., toward the sphere outside the id-ego conflicts. Although he did not intend his theoretical findings to have a direct impact on the practice of psychoanalysis, their indirect consequences for the analysts' technical attitudes were considerable.

So far as my personal contributions go, I was wholly identified with the ventures into defense analysis. In fact, in *The Ego and the Mechanisms of Defense* (1936), I was already leaning heavily in this direction.

The second of the suggested remedies is of a different nature.

When Freud wrote of *earliest* defensive struggles or of analyzing the prehistory of the oedipus complex, what he had in mind, probably, were events of the anal and oral phases, the period immediately after ego and id had separated off from each other. There is little or no evidence that he thought it possible to deal therapeutically with preverbal experience, in spite of his knowledge and conviction that this is an all-important period in the individual's life when essential lines for development are laid down, when reaction patterns are preformed, and when basic deprivations and frustrations exert an influence which threatens to be lasting.[5]

Departing from this position, a considerable cross-section of the psychoanalytic community today pins their faith on the analysis of the first year of life, with the purpose of therapeutically modifying the impact of the earliest happenings. Freud's discovery that every neurosis of the adult is preceded by an infantile neurosis and that the latter has to be analyzed before the former can be reached, is paraphrased by them as follows: every infantile neurosis in the oedipal period is preceded by fateful interactions between infant and mother in the very first days and months of life, and it is this archaic, preverbal phase which has to be revived in the transference and analyzed before the later infantile neurosis can be approached effectively.

This view is held today by many analysts of otherwise widely divergent opinions.[6] Interestingly enough, it has been described systematically, not by a member of one of the more independent and revolutionary analytic sections, but by Jeanne Lampl-de Groot. In a recent paper "On Obstacles Standing in the Way of Psychoanalytic Cure"

[5] See also M. Balint (1958) on "basic faults."
[6] See, for example René Spitz, D. W. Winnicott, Melanie Klein, Herbert Rosenfeld, and others.

(1967), she goes through the list of difficulties cited by Freud, referring each back to some happening during the earliest mother-infant interaction: the (masochistic) *negative therapeutic reaction* of some patients who have a need for self-punishment, to "the primitive fear of their own aggressive drives and the destruction of their omnipotence fantasies" directed against the mother; the *incapacity to tame the instinctual drives*, to the modes of drive discharge initiated when the ego is helpless vis-à-vis the drives and "strongly dependent on the mother's support"; *irregular and distorted ego development*, to failures in the original dyad between infant and mother; the *bisexual problems*, to the infant's fear of merging with a dominating mother, a fear of passivity which later, in the phallic phase, acquires sexual meaning.

Any attempt to carry analysis from the verbal to the preverbal period of development brings with it practical and technical innovations as well as theoretical implications, many of which are controversial.

What strikes the observer first is a change in the type of *psychic material* with which the analysis is dealing. Instead of exploring the disharmonies between the various agencies within a structured personality, the analyst is concerned with the events which lead from the chaotic, undifferentiated state toward the initial building up of a psychic structure. This means going beyond the area of intrapsychic conflict, which had always been the legitimate target for psychoanalysis, and into the darker area of interaction between innate endowment and environmental influence. The implied aim is to undo or to counteract the impact of the very forces on which the rudiments of personality development are based.

Analysts who work for this aim assure us that this can be achieved. They feel enthusiastic about the new therapeutic prospects which they see opening out before them. Jeanne Lampl-de Groot, in her paper, confesses to being "far from optimistic" in cases in which the damage done during the initial mother-infant interaction has been massive. I myself cannot help feeling doubtful about trying to advance into the area of primary repression, i.e., to deal with processes which, by nature, are totally different from the results of the ego's defensive maneuvers with which we feel familiar.

As regards *technique*, it is obvious that different methods are needed for the approach to the earliest rather than to the later phases. Lampl-de Groot mentions "nonverbal modes of communication" which become unavoidable. Others speak of "silent communion" between analyst and patient, or use other terms to stress the need for the analyst's intuitive understanding of the patient's signs and signals, his empathy, etc. However that may be, there is no doubt that neither memory nor verbal recall reach into the depth of postnatal, preverbal experience. Therefore, remembering yields its place to repetition, verbal communication to re-enactment. This explains the heightened significance of communication via the transference in many present-day analyses, where transference interpretations are considered the only therapeutically effective ones and where the transference phenomena are perforce given preference over memory, free association, and dreams, as the only real road to the unconscious.

It is, in fact, this central and unique role given to the transference in the psychoanalytic process, to the exclusion of all other avenues of communication, which is, to date, one of the points of controversy in the analytic world. There is, further, the question whether the transference really has the power to transport the patient back as far as the beginning of life. Many are convinced that this is the case. Others, I among them, raise the point that it is one thing for preformed, object-related fantasies to return from repression and be redirected from the inner to the outer world (i.e., to the person of the analyst); but that it is an entirely different, almost magical expectation to have the patient in analysis change back into the prepsychological, undifferentiated, and unstructured state, in which no divisions exist between body and mind or self and object.

The argument that it is the quality of the analytic setting itself which promotes such deep regressions also does not necessarily command belief. In many respects, the mother-infant and the analyst-patient relationship are dissimilar rather than similar. What is characteristic for the former is the infant's need for an ever-present, exclusive, timelessly devoted, giving, and comforting partner, while the latter is characterized by the existence of rivals, restriction in time, demands for punctuality and cooperation, release of anxiety, withholding of reassurance, frustration of wishes, at best token gratifications. Taken altogether, the question is left open whether, in fact, the re-enactment of life after birth does, or does not, take place in the patient's mind.

Another controversial point concerns the role of the ego within the analytic process. In the classical procedure, as described above, this role is considered decisive in various respects: for the initial pact with the analyst; for the patient's willingness to reduce or suspend defenses and thereby promote upsurges from the id; for accepting insight; for incorporating the result of interpretations within its own organization, etc. Furthermore, the aim itself of analysis is geared to the concept of a mediating ego that is helped to abandon defensive structures built up in infantile life on faulty premises and to replace them by more adequate and rational solutions.

Perhaps it has never been spelled out explicitly that such considerations cease to apply where analysis aims to penetrate into pre-ego strata, where the power of a quasi-delusional transference is meant to carry the patient far beyond the confines of ego functioning into the reliving of primary emotional experience. What is expected of the ego under these altered circumstances is not only the undoing of its own faulty moves but also the undoing of the impact of the very processes which have led to its formation.

More important than these mainly technical considerations seem to me *two theoretical assumptions* which are implied in them.

The first of these is a revision of the distinction between inherited and acquired characteristics. According to Freud (1937), "We have no reason to dispute the existence and importance of original, innate distinguishing characteristics of the ego" (p. 240), which, is, after all, initially, one with the id. Nevertheless, the extent of an individual's innate endowment has been under dispute in recent years, based partly on psychoanalytic reconstructions, partly on the direct observation of mother-child couples. Both types of data have produced in us the conviction that much that used to be considered innate can now be shown to have been acquired during the first year of life and to have been added to the inherited constitution.[7]

[7] On this point see also Martin James (1960) and others.

But if there is unanimous agreement on this point, there is, in contrast, vivid disagreement concerning a theoretical inference drawn from it. The new technical proposals aimed at the beginning of life imply the assumption that whatever is acquired is reversible. This is by no means proved. It may well be that the very basis on which personality formation rests is, in fact, bedrock.

THE ANALYST

That the smoothness of the analytic process is interfered with not only by the patients' resistances and negative reactions but also by flaws in the analysts' abilities and personalities belongs to basic knowledge. It has come under scrutiny at all times under various titles such as a general lack of sensitivity to the unconscious, blind spots due to the analyst's own repressions, countertransference reactions, etc. In "Analysis Terminable and Interminable" Freud mentioned as unfortunate for the outcome of analysis if the analyst does not possess "a considerable degree of mental normality and correctness," "some kind of superiority," a basic "love of truth" (p. 248). He alerted analysts to the danger of having their own instinctual demands stirred up by constant preoccupation with the patients' repressed material and then either strengthening their defenses by diverting "the implications and demands of analysis from themselves" or by permitting themselves in action the freedom which they grant to their patients in free thought and association.

Jeanne Lampl-de Groot (1967), following René Spitz (1965), lays special stress on the need for intactness of the analyst's receptive empathy, a mode of functioning which is frequently blocked early in life, by repression of the resentment caused by the mother's interference with the infant's "need to become a person in his own right" (p. 32). The harmful consequences of unchecked counter-transference have been emphasized by many authors, Paula Heimann (1950) foremost among them. That only the analyst's own preparatory analysis can combat these defects is a general opinion, although only Freud (1937) carried this conviction far enough to recommend that "Every analyst should periodically—at intervals of five years or so—submit himself to analysis once more, without feeling ashamed of taking this step" (p. 249).

In addition to these time-honored concerns about the analysts' therapeutic activities, new ones have recently come into the foreground with regard to the analysts' literary output and the impact of the quality of these publications on the future of psychoanalysis. In some quarters, notably in the American Psychoanalytic Association, these have been taken so seriously that an "Ad Hoc Committee for Scientific Activities"[8] has been set up to explore the situation. An official Report (1967) of this Committee emphasizes that "while there exists a good deal of productive investigative activity in the peripheral and applied fields, there is deficiency of creative research in the central areas of psychoanalysis, which, if it is not remedied, might in the long run constitute a threat to the survival of psychoanalysis as a science." Discussing the central areas of psychoanalysis, Heinz Kohut stresses that among the contributions to man's understanding of himself, "what is

[8] Members: Heinz Kohut, Chairman; A. Russell Anderson, Grete L. Bibring, Douglas D. Bond, John E. Gedo, Seymour L. Lustman, Peter B. Neubauer.

specific for analysis is that the increase in knowledge and the subsequent potential increase in mastery (1) concern the inner life of man, and (2) are the result of an expansion of the territory of the ego, i.e., specifically due to transformations from infantile forms of automatic pain avoidance to tension tolerance and reality acceptance."[9]

In the face of the dangers which are foreseen, not for the extension but for the intensification of the psychoanalytic theory, the Committee members make suggestions how to promote *creative research, scientific progress,* and *productivity* among analysts. They also raise the question whether whatever is lacking in these respects in the present analytic scene is due to the methods of selecting candidates for analytic training (in the United States: restriction to medically trained individuals with the exclusion of potentially creative minds from allied fields); or to the training methods themselves (which have become institutionalized and are, on the whole, restricted to matters of technique and therapy); or to the general atmosphere in the analytic communities (where professional success and advancement are often priced more highly than patient scientific exploration).

Although I personally find it easy to identify wholeheartedly with the aims and objects of this Committee, the answers with which I myself come up are of a different nature. I do not believe that either selection or training methods, or society trends can severely interfere with creativity. There has been a profusion of creative minds in modern medicine, even if in the organic field; moreover, creative individuals are usually the revolutionary ones whose

[9] From a letter to Douglas Bond, June 3, 1967. Quoted with the writer's permission. See also Kohut (1970).

spirits are not easily subdued by whatever is imposed on them, first by their teachers, later by their professional colleagues. Besides, it may be an error altogether to think of these developments in terms of creativity. The analyst's task is not to create, i.e., to invent anything, but to observe, to explore, to understand, and to explain. It is in respect to these latter activities that an important quality appears to me in danger of getting lost.

Psychoanalytic thinking, in classical terms, implied the specific demand that every clinical fact should be approached from four aspects: *genetically*, as to its origin; *dynamically*, as to the interplay of forces of which it is the result; *economically*, with regard to its energy charge; *topographically* (later *structurally*), concerning its localization within the mental apparatus.[10] It was the psychology based on this view of mental functioning which was singled out by the name of *metapsychology*.

Nevertheless, in our times, the term metapsychology has assumed a very different meaning. What it denotes now is largely theory building, distant from the area of clinical material, an activity which demands and is reserved for a specific, speculative quality of mind. As such it has become the bugbear of the clinically oriented analyst who feels wholly divorced from it. This brings about a division which, in the long run, threatens both areas with sterility: the theoretical field, due to the absence of clinical data; the clinical field, due to a diminution in their theoretical evaluation and exploration. What is lost, finally, is what used to be considered as a *sine qua non* in psychoanalysis: the essential *unity* between clinical and theoretical thinking.

[10] A fifth aspect, the *adaptive* one to be added later; see Hartmann (1939) and Rapaport and Gill (1959).

A look at the history of the four metapsychological aspects may take us a step further. Although they were meant to exist and be developed simultaneously, this did not happen according to intention. There were always periods when one or the other of them gained ascendancy to the comparative detriment of the remaining ones.

The first to be given widespread approval was, no doubt, the *dynamic* aspect. In fact, to approach mental functioning and mental illness in terms of conflict between opposing forces seemed so obvious and acceptable, not only to the analysts themselves, that for a while it dominated the scene and became the hallmark of enlightened thinking, especially in psychiatry. On this basis, psychoanalysis used to be alluded to as a "dynamic psychology." This, of course, disregarded the fact that in metapsychological thinking an interplay of internal forces as such remains inconclusive unless information is added where in the mental apparatus these forces are localized; whether they possess the same or different psychical qualities (unconscious, preconscious, conscious); whether they are able to meet each other on the same level and within the same mental area; to reduce each other; to enter into compromises with each other, etc.; or whether they are walled off from each other by defensive activity. In short, the dynamic point of view is not profitable for the analyst, except in combination with the *topographical* one. But acceptance of the latter was more hesitant and less wholehearted and did not become prominent in the analytic literature until 1926 when *Inhibitions, Symptoms and Anxiety* put it into the foreground in its revised form as the "*structural* aspect."

There was never any doubt about psychoanalysis as a *genetic* psychology. The genetic point of view had a recognized existence from the moment when psychoanalytic exploration turned from the neurotic problems of adult life to their forerunners in childhood and demonstrated the impact of early on later happenings and patterns.

In contrast, the *economic* aspect had a chequered career and not only because "the term 'mental energy' may give rise to criticism on the part of psychologists, psychiatrists, and psychoanalysts" (Lampl-de Groot, 1967, p. 24). Freud himself was always convinced of the highly important part quantity plays in the defensive struggles against unpleasure which go on in the mental apparatus early in life and play havoc with the normality of the ego. He was equally convinced of the fact that the outcome of every analytic treatment depends essentially on quantitative factors, i.e., on the strength of the patient's resistances and negative reactions measured against the amounts of energy upon which analysis can draw. Nevertheless, he admitted with regret that "our theoretical concepts have neglected to attach the same importance to the *economic* line of approach as they have to the *dynamic* and *topographical* ones" (1937, p. 226f.).

To return from here to the analysts of today and the problems of present and future development of analytic thinking:

What may give rise to concern is a comparative neglect of the fact that the relations of the four metapsychological aspects to the notion of a psychoanalytic cure are not on an equal level. While alterations of the economics, dynamics, and structure of the patient's personality are the essence of analytic therapy, exploration of the genetic roots is not the aim in itself, but is the means to the end of understanding and interpretation. Heinz Hartmann, who in psychoanalysis is the genetic explorer par excellence, expressed this very succinctly when in 1939 he wrote concerning his own efforts to disentangle the roots of ego development: "Many of these lengthy . . . considerations are not psychoanalytic in the narrow sense, and some of them seem to have taken us quite far from the core of psychoanalysis" (p. 108).

However that may be, one look at the analytic scene of today can convince us that the desire to unearth ever earlier and deeper antecedents, not only of the ego but of human emotions, anxieties, and struggles in general, has taken hold of the analysts' imagination. For the moment it outstrips most other interests, and it may take some time until the other metapsychological aspects catch up again with the genetic one, which has strayed ahead.

But this, exactly, is what we should be waiting for. The newly discovered facts about early and earliest life need to fall into place within the dynamics, the economy, and the structure of the personalities for which they prepare the ground. Only in this way can metapsychology regain its former status. It is also only in this way that we shall approach once more what the Ad Hoc Committee for Scientific Activities calls hopefully

"a creative era in psychoanalysis."

10

The Symptomatology of Childhood: A Preliminary Attempt at Classification (1970)

THE MISLEADING QUALITY OF MANIFEST SYMPTOMATOLOGY

Analysts have always been proud of the distinction that theirs is a causal therapy, aiming directly at the conflicts and stresses which are hidden in the patients' personalities and underlie their symptomatology. Inevitably, with this approach they find themselves at cross-purposes with many of the adult neurotics under analysis who are intent only on being relieved of the suffering caused by painful anxi-

Presented to the Western New England Psychoanalytic Society, New Haven, Conn., on April 18, 1970. First published in *The Psychoanalytic Study of the Child*, 25:19-41, 1970.

eties and crippling obsessions, and who regard these as the only logical starting point for investigation; or with the parents of child patients who are concerned only with removing the disturbing manifestations in the child and completely disregard the pathological turn in the child's development which is revealed by the disturbances that trouble them.

Naturally, neither the adult neurotics themselves nor the parents of these endangered children possess the analyst's knowledge of the deceiving nature of overt symptomatology. They lack the experience of how quickly anxieties can be shifted from one apparently all-important object to another; or how easily one particular compulsion can be substituted for by a different one. Therefore, they cannot appreciate that symptoms are no more than symbols, to be taken merely as indications that some mental turmoil is taking place in the lower strata of the mind. Many symptoms, important and unassailable as they seem if untreated, give way fairly easily to many types of therapy. But if they are removed by measures which do not reach to their roots, their place may be taken almost instantaneously by other pathological formations which, although overtly different, express the same latent content and may be no less aggravating for the individual's life.

On the other hand, symptoms are negligible in the analyst's view only for the purposes of the technique of therapy; in their eyes, too, symptoms have retained full significance so far as diagnostic classification is concerned. Whether a patient is assessed as a hysteric or phobic subject, as suffering from an obsessional neurosis or a paranoid state, is decided wholly on the basis of his manifest symptomatology, i.e., on the overt evidence of bodily conversions, anxiety attacks, avoidance mechanisms, compulsive acts, rumina-tions, projections, etc.

There is an incongruity here between the analyst's thera-peutic thinking, which is metapsychological, i.e., directed toward the dynamic, economic, genetic, and structural as-pects of psychic functioning, and his thinking as a diagnos-tician, which proceeds on the basis of concepts and categories which are descriptive.[1] The difference between these view-points is so fundamental that it has caused many analysts to withdraw their interest altogether from diagnostic assess-ment as from an area which is neither essential nor very significant for their field of work, and has caused some others to regard all their patients' abnormalities as mere variations of the many vagaries and complexities of human behavior.[2]

But before subscribing to a diagnostic nihilism of this extreme kind, the attempt seems worthwhile to bridge the gap between the two contrasting approaches and to use the vast array of overt symptoms themselves for the pur-pose of forging links between them. There is no reason, after all, why the very classification of symptomatology should not go beyond enumeration and description and why probing into dynamic clashes and genetic antecedents should be excluded from it, to be reserved for scrutiny within the analytic procedure. It is inevitable, of course, that such a different mode of classification will sacrifice the neatness and order of any system based on phenomenology.

[1] Or, at best, on the basis of unconscious content converted into conscious symbols.

[2] An outstanding example of the latter is Karl Menninger who is known to condemn all psychiatric labels and classifications as un-justified offenses against the patient's human dignity, i.e., as "name-calling."

It is only to be expected that in many instances there will be no one-to-one correlation between underlying unconscious constellation and manifest symptom. The former, as shown in Part I of this paper, can give rise to a variety of manifestations; the latter, as demonstrated in Part II, are the result of a variety of causes. Far from this being confusing for the analyst, it can only help to sharpen his diagnostic acumen.

When one is dealing with the psychopathology of childhood, a descriptive survey of symptomatology is even less rewarding. As is well known, in the immature personality isolated symptoms are no reliable guide to any specific type of underlying pathology, nor are they a measure of its severity. Symptoms may be no more than the child's answer to some developmental stress and as such transitory, i.e., liable to pass away together with the maturational phase which has given rise to them. Or symptoms may represent a permanent countercathexis against some threatening drive derivative and as such be crippling to further development. Or symptoms, though pathological in origin, may nevertheless be ego-syntonic, and merged with the structure of the child's personality to a degree which makes it difficult to distinguish between such manifestations as outward evidence of ongoing pathological involvement or as more or less normal, stable features of the individual's character. There is no doubt that in any classification system based on phenomenology, these widely different classes of symptom appear as if on a par.

Moreover, if we scrutinize what children's clinics list under the heading of "referral symptoms," we feel doubtful whether in all instances these manifestations deserve to be classified as symptomatology, or whether the meaning of the term "symptom" is not extended here beyond its proper use. What is grouped together in such surveys are, on the one hand, the true signs or residues of present or past pathological processes; on the other hand, such complaints by parents and disruptions of the child's life as, for example, multiplicity of fears; disturbances of intake, digestion, and elimination; sleep, respiratory or skin disturbances; aches and pains, motor disturbances; unusual sexual behavior; self-injurious acts and habits; disturbances of mood, affect, and object relatedness; failure of learning processes and/or poor quality of other ego functions; behavior disorders including antisocial reactions; moral indifference; failures of adaptation; failure to comply with parental demands or to fulfill parental expectation in general; etc.

Although an enumeration of this kind promises a first orientation in the field, and seems to satisfy the clinicians' immediate need at the stage of intake of cases, what it does, in fact, is to defeat its own purpose. By remaining strictly on the descriptive level, regardless of genetic roots, dynamic, structural, and economic complications, such an initial approach discourages analytic thinking and blocks the road to diagnostic assessment proper instead of facilitating it. Last but not least, it provides no clue for the diagnostician with regard to the choice of adequate therapeutic method.[3]

There is no warning implied in such a phenomenological survey that many of the items listed in it may belong genetically to any one of two, three, or more analytic categories. A *behavior disorder*, such as lying, for example, may be rooted in the child's stage of ego development, i.e., express the immature individual's inability to distinguish between

[3] This may be the explanation why many clinics for children provide only one type of treatment, i.e., once weekly psychotherapy.

reality and fantasy, or may signify a delay in acquiring and perfecting this important ego function. But, equally, lying may betray the level and quality of the child's object relations and express his fear of punishment and loss of love. As fantasy lying, it may be evidence of persistent denial of unpalatable realities, with the function of reality testing fundamentally intact. As a feature of the child's character, it may denote weakness or failure of superego function.[4]

Disturbance of elimination such as extreme withholding of feces may have its roots in a very early vulnerability of the digestive system (i.e., psychosomatic); or it may be symbolic of the child's imitation of and identification with a pregnant mother (hysterical); or it may signify his revolt against inappropriate forms of toilet training (behavioral); or it may express phallic sexual needs and fantasies on a regressed anal level (obsessional).

Similarly, *enuresis* may be the sign either of simple failure of control in a generally impulsive personality structure,[5] or a highly complex reaction on the level of penis envy and castration anxiety.

Learning failures may point to developmental arrest or, conversely, to blocking and inhibitions interfering with basically intact intellectual functions.

Antisocial reactions, such as aggressive outbursts, may be the mark of defusion or insufficient fusion between libido and aggression; or of insufficient control of drives in an impulsive character; or of a violent defensive reaction against underlying passive-feminine leanings in boys striving overtly for masculinity.

[4] See also Hedy Schwarz, "On Lying" (unpublished manuscript).
[5] See J. J. Michaels (1955).

In short, manifest symptoms may be identical so far as their appearance is concerned, but may differ widely in respect to latent meaning and pathological significance. According to the latter, they may require very different types of therapeutic handling.

Ideally, the solution for the analytic clinician in the children's field is a classification of symptoms which, on the one hand, embodies consideration of the various metapsychological aspects, while, on the other hand, maintains links with and pointers to the descriptive diagnostic categories as they are in common use. It is obvious, nevertheless, that no complex system of this kind will lend itself to the quick, almost automatic application to which diagnosticians are used so long as they remain within the framework of phenomenology. What is needed to make such a new classification of symptomatology profitable is, already at the diagnostic stage, a thorough investigation of the child's personality which makes it possible to pinpoint each symptom's relevance with regard to developmental level, structure, dynamic significance, etc.

I. SYMPTOMATOLOGY PROPER

As indicated above, for a first attempt of ordering the clinical material, it seems useful to separate symptoms, in the narrow sense of the term, from other signs of disturbance and other reasons for a child's referral for diagnosis and treatment. In this restricted field it becomes more possible to survey the relevant range of pathological processes and to correlate them with the various forms of mental illnesses which correspond to them.

1. Symptoms Resulting from Initial Nondifferentiation between Somatic and Psychological Processes: Psychosomatics

At the beginning of life, before somatic and psychological processes are separated off from each other, bodily excitations such as hunger, cold, pain, etc., are discharged as easily via mental pathways in the form of unpleasure, anxiety, anger, rage, as mental upsets of any kind are discharged via disturbances of the body surface, of intake, digestion, elimination, breathing, etc. Such "psychosomatic" reactions are developmentally determined at this time of life. It is important for later events which particular bodily outlets are given preference by the individual since this choice gives rise to increased sensitivity and vulnerability in the organ system concerned, i.e., the skin, the respiratory system, the intestinal system, the sleep rhythm, etc.

Normally, this easy access from mind to body (and vice versa) diminishes with advancing ego development and the opening up of new, purely mental pathways of discharge by means of action, thought, speech. Where it remains more than usually open, on the other hand, it accounts directly for the range of *psychosomatic symptomatology*, i.e., for *asthma, eczema, ulcerative colitis, headaches, migraine*, etc.

It is also responsible for the creation of the so-called "somatic compliance" which, in later and more complex hysterical symptom formation, facilitates the conversion of mental processes into physical manifestations with symbolic meaning.

2. Symptoms Resulting from Compromise Formations between Id and Ego: Neurotic Symptomatology

Since basic psychoanalytic training takes place in the area of theory and therapy of the neuroses, analysts feel most knowledgeable about the specific structure of neurotic symptomatology. In fact, so far as the neuroses are concerned, the term "symptom" has become synonymous with the conception of the ego acting as intermediary and finding solutions for the clashes between drive derivatives on the one hand and other, rational or moral, claims of the individual on the other hand. The complex route of symptom formation along a line of danger-anxiety-regression-defense-compromise has become familiar.

The resulting symptomatic structures may prove ego-dystonic and continue to produce mental pain and discomfort; or they may be accepted as ego-syntonic and become part of the individual's character. The latter outcome depends largely on economic factors, i.e., on the varying degrees to which elements from id, ego, and superego sides are embodied in the final symptomatic result. It depends also on the ego's willingness to become distorted itself by accommodating the pathological manifestation within its structure. This last-mentioned solution, not to treat the symptoms as a foreign body, is one often adopted by children.

Since compromise formations of this kind depend for their existence on established boundaries between id and ego, unconscious and conscious, we do not expect to find neurotic symptoms in the unstructured personality, i.e., in early infancy. Neurotic symptom formation waits until the ego has divided itself off from the id, but does not need to wait until ego and superego also have become two independent agencies. The first id-ego conflicts, and with them the first neurotic symptoms as conflict solutions, are produced with the ego under pressure from the environment, i.e., threatened not by guilt feelings arising internally from the superego but by dangers arising from the object world such as loss of love, rejection, punishment.

The neurotic manifestations of this phase are *hysterical* in nature so far as the body areas involved have oral or oral-aggressive value and the symptom implies a primitive defense against these drive representatives (*affection of single limbs, motor disturbances, aches and pains, food fads and avoidances, vomiting*). They are *obsessional* in nature so far as they defend against anal-sadistic strivings (first appearance of *compulsive cleanliness, orderliness, repetitiveness, avoidance of touch*).

With the emergence and dissolution of the phallic-oedipal strivings and the superego as an independent source of guilt these isolated symptoms become organized into the syndromes which form the familiar infantile neuroses, i.e., the full-blown *phobias* (of animals, of separation, of doctor, dentist, of the lavatory, of school, etc.) as well as the true *obsessional neuroses*, complete with *doubting, repeating, rituals,* bedtime *ceremonials, ruminations, compulsive actions.* Crippling *inhibitions, ego restrictions,* and *self-injurious tendencies* appear as character defenses against aggression at this time.

3. Symptoms Resulting from the Irruption of Id Derivatives into the Ego

Neurotic symptomatology comes about only where the border between id and ego is intact. This may be lacking for a variety of reasons: the ego may be constitutionally weak; or the id strivings may be constitutionally increased in intensity; damage may have been done to the ego through traumatic events which have put it out of action; or through phase-determined alterations of the inner equilibrium. In any case, the result will be failure to control id content and the entrance of id elements into the ego organization, with disruptive consequences for the latter.

Where the irrupting elements are part of primary process functioning and take the place of the rational secondary process thinking which is characteristic for the ego otherwise, the corresponding manifest symptoms such as *disturbances of thought and language, misidentifications, delusions,* etc., are significant for the differential diagnosis between neurosis and psychosis; if only partially in evidence, they are a hallmark of the borderline states between the two diagnostic categories.

Where the irrupting elements are from the area of the drives, the resulting symptoms consist of the *undefended* (or unsuccessfully defended) *acting out of drive derivatives* with disregard for reality considerations which is characteristic for certain types of delinquency and criminality.

The combination of both leakages from the id produces those ominous types of abnormal behavior which, on the one hand, carry the individual beyond the confines of what is legally permissible and, on the other hand, characterize him as mentally ill and for this reason absolved from responsibility for his actions.

4. Symptoms Resulting from Changes in the Libido Economy or Direction of Cathexis

Although all symptom formation implies pathological up-sets to the dynamics and structural aspects of the person-ality, these may be secondary to alterations in the economy of the libido and the direction of its employment.

Where, for example, the narcissistic cathexis of the self is increased unduly, the corresponding symptomatic results are *egotism, self-centeredness, overvaluation* of the self, in extreme cases *megalomania.* Where such cathexis is de-creased unduly, the symptoms are *bodily neglect, self-dero-gation, inferiority feelings, depressive states, depersonaliza-tion* (in childhood).

Direction of cathexis may be altered in three respects with corresponding symptomatology. Narcissistic libido may move from the individual's mind to his body, where the increased cathexis of specific body parts creates *hypo-chondriacal* symptoms. Object libido may be withdrawn from the external world, changed into narcissistic libido, and employed wholly in cathexis of the self. Or, conversely, all narcissistic libido may be added to the existing object libido and become concentrated on an external love object with consequences for its overvaluation; in extreme cases, for complete *emotional surrender* to it.

5. Symptoms Resulting from Changes in the Quality or Direction of Aggression

What is significant for symptomatology in this respect are the changes in intensity as well as the frequent changes in aim direction, from mind to body, from self to object, and vice versa.

The former, the quantitative changes, are brought about mainly by the vagaries within the defense organization, in childhood by the varying quality of the defense mechanisms which are employed, from crudely primitive to highly sophisticated. These decide about the availability or non-availability of the necessary aggressive contributions to ego functioning and to sublimations. Some of the resulting symptomatic manifestations are *inhibitions* and *failure* in play, learning, and work.

The type of defense used against aggression is also responsible for the swings between *self-injurious behavior,* which corresponds to aggression turned against the self, and violent *aggressive-destructive outbursts* against animate and inanimate objects in the environment.

6. Symptoms Resulting from Undefended Regressions

In our work with children we have become alerted to a type of pathological manifestation which equals a prestage of neurotic symptom formation, but remains abortive so far as the infantile neuroses are concerned. Its point of origin is the phallic phase, its precipitating cause is danger and anxiety arising from the oedipus and castration complexes, followed by regression to oral and anal fixation points.

While in neurotic symptom formation such regressions are rejected by the ego and defended against, in these cases they are accepted and treated as ego-syntonic; i.e., they do not give rise to further conflict. The result is a lowering of all aspects of the personality (drive activity as well as ego functioning). The clinical pictures which correspond to this are *infantilism* and a form of *pseudodebility*, accompanied by behavioral symptoms such as *whining, clinging,* prolonged *dependency, passive-feminine traits* in boys, *inefficiency,* etc.

7. Symptoms Resulting from Organic Causes

The foregoing enumeration leaves to the last those disturbances of psychic function which have an organic origin such as brain damage due to prenatal influences or to birth injury or to later inflammatory processes or to traumatic accidents. A whole range of symptoms is attributable to these causes such as a *delay in developmental milestones, difficulties in locomotion,* difficulties with *speech, poor* quality of *intellectual functions, interference with concentration, flatness or lability of affect, distractability,* etc. Many of these symptoms bear a close resemblance to the result of inhibitions, compromise formations, or any other of the categories described above, and the correct diagnosis is difficult in those cases where the neurological tests prove inconclusive. Doubtless, mistakes in differential diagnosis occur here in both directions, either mental or organic damage being discounted unjustifiably, or a combination between both factors being overlooked.

What should also be added here are those symptomatic manifestations or deviations from the norm which are the direct or indirect consequence of physical handicaps, whether inborn or acquired ones. It is well known by now that where vision is missing, ego development is thrown into confusion, the balance between autoerotism and object relatedness disturbed, aggression inhibited, passivity enhanced, etc. Where hearing is absent or grossly defective, not only speech development but secondary process thinking and, with it, higher development of the personality are interfered with. Missing limbs, spasticity bring with them their own psychopathology which needs to be explored further.

II. OTHER SIGNS OF DISTURBANCE AND OTHER REASONS FOR A CHILD'S CLINICAL REFERRAL

As discussed before, not all the manifestations which lead to a child's clinical examination are evidence of true pathology, nor do they all form part of recognized clinical pictures. There are other disturbances, upsets, and malfunctions, and, consequently, other reasons for referral. What they all have in common is that they represent interferences with normal processes, with adequate growth and development, with reasonable behavior, with contentment and enjoyment of life, with adaptation to environmental conditions and requirements. Since the causes for them are diffuse, and the same overt manifestation may be due to a variety of underlying constellations, the attempt seems justified to approach their classification from a different angle. The method adopted before consisted of following certain psychic processes ongoing in the depth to their various expressions on the surface of the mind. The procedure applied to what follows is the opposite one, namely, to start out from the surface signs of disturbance and, from there, to trace back the links to whichever upheaval, involvement or failure may be responsible for them.

1. The Fears and Anxieties

The mere number of children who are referred to clinics with fears and anxieties of all kinds and intensities justifies the attempt to classify these manifestations as such, i.e., apart from the active role which they play in the formation of a variety of clinical syndromes.

It is well known to analysts, of course, that anxiety, experienced by the ego, is a regular accompaniment to development in childhood, occasioned on the one hand by the helplessness of the immature being, on the other hand by structuralization, higher development, and the resultant rising tension between the inner agencies. Its absence rather than its presence in the picture is considered an ominous sign. Nevertheless, even though anxiety is normal and the disturbance in many instances no more than a quantitative exacerbation of expectable reactions, anxiety states remain one of the most common and potent causes of suffering in childhood.

To arrive at their understanding, these manifestations have to be viewed from a number of angles. For example, their classification can be, and has been, attempted from the *developmental* point of view, by creating a chronological sequence according to which the common fears and anxieties are allocated to the various instinctual phases in which they arise and, connected with these, the external or internal dangers toward which they are directed. Classification has also been carried out from the aspect of *dynamic* vicissitudes, i.e., from the side of the defenses employed to keep fear and anxiety in check, and the *economic* factors which determine the success or failure of these coping mechanisms. What has been done most frequently by analytic authors, without doubt, is to explore the role played by the various kinds of anxiety in *structural* conflict and the responsibility which has to be ascribed to them for the swings between mental health and illness, since it is at their instigation that the ego's defensive mechanisms and, following on them, the ego's compromises with the id are put into action.

Obviously, it is the diagnostician's task to explore each of these avenues in greater detail.

(i) THE CHRONOLOGY OF FEARS AND ANXIETIES

Where the clinician arrives at ordering the child's manifest fears and anxieties according to the developmental stages in which they arise and according to the dangers represented by these stages, many of the quantitative increases in them can be understood as due to unsatisfied developmental needs or to, unjustifiable developmental interferences (see Nagera, 1966).

The initial stages of ego development, in this view, become correlated with the so-called *archaic fears* of the infant. These are inevitable while the ego has no resources of its own to cope either with the massive stimuli which arrive from the environment or with the equally disturbing tensions in the inner world. These fears increase in intensity and range when a child's ego is unusually sensitive or when a child's mother is unusually unable to provide the comfort and reassurance to which the infant is entitled at this stage. Where ego development is slow, the archaic fears last beyond infancy. Their undue persistence and prominence can be taken as diagnostic indicators for retardation or arrest in the area of ego functioning.

The symbiotic stage, i.e., the phase of biological unity between infant and mother, is relevant for the arousal of *separation anxiety*, i.e., fear of object loss, whenever this unity is threatened. Separation anxiety becomes overwhelming if the infant experiences actual separations from the mother, or if in other ways the mother proves unreliable as a stable object. Separation anxiety can be prolonged unduly, which points diagnostically to fixation in the symbiotic phase or arrests in it.[6]

When the parental objects become representatives of the demand for drive control, the child's difficulty of complying with this arouses *fear of rejection* by the object and fear of the loss of the object's love. As such, these fears are signs of beginning moral adjustment and positive prestages of superego development; their nonemergence points to developmental failure in these respects. They become excessive for environmental reasons if the parents commit errors in either the timing or the harshness of their demands. But even where no blame can be attached to the environment in this respect, oversensitivity of the ego or excessive dependency on being loved can bring about the same result for internal reasons.

The arrival of a boy in the phallic phase, which as such is a welcome event, commonly reveals itself at the same time in a heightened fear for the intactness of his sex organ, i.e., in *castration anxiety*. The frequent exacerbations of this correspond directly to the strivings of the oedipus com-

---

[6] There are fears of object loss in later childhood which manifest themselves as difficulties in separating from the parental objects, especially the mother. Although phenomenologically identical, they are different in dynamic and structural respects, i.e., due to internal rejection of aggression and death wishes directed against the parents.

plex and depend on the defenses and compromise formations which the ego employs to deal with them. Castration anxiety represents a specific threat for development owing to the drive regressions initiated by it and their further role for neurosis and character formation.

The child's first moves from family to community and his new dependency on the opinions of his peers give rise to an additional *fear*, that of *social disgrace*, which is especially experienced in school.

According to the individual child's structural development, i.e., with the establishment of the superego's independence and authority (whenever this happens), the advance from anxiety to *guilt* is made as the crowning step in this chronology of infantile fears.

Obviously, such a chronology of fears and anxieties is helpful as a diagnostic tool since observation of the presenting disturbance leads directly to the corresponding phase of development in which the child's mental upset is rooted. Nevertheless, it fails to serve the diagnostician in other respects, since it does not include an important anxiety which neither originates in any particular phase nor bears the characteristics of any one, but persists through the whole period of development and reappears at all times of later life, not for reasons of fixation or regression but whenever the inner structural balance is upset. This anxiety denotes the ego's concern for the intactness of its own organization, at whatever level; it is due to economic reasons, i.e., to the uneven distribution of energy between id and ego; and it gains in intensity whenever the strength of the drive derivatives increases or ego strength diminishes for some reason.

In contrast to other anxeties, this *fear of the id* is not favorably influenced by the lightening of external pressure. Much to the parents' disappointment, it is increased rather than decreased by excessive educational leniency or by educational nihilism.

When fear of the id is more than usually in evidence, it arouses the diagnostic suspicion of a borderline or prepsychotic state.

(ii) THE MANIFEST AND LATENT CONTENT
OF FEARS AND ANXIETIES

While in the childhood cases described, the affect of anxiety is manifest and brought directly to the clinician's notice, the latent meaning of the fear is obscured by the fact that almost any type of anxiety can find symbolic expression in almost any mental representation, or can remain free-floating and unattached. Nevertheless, in most instances it is possible to correlate fear and symbol as follows:

Archaic fears:	of darkness, noise, strangers, solitude, etc.
separation anxiety:	of annihilation, starvation, loneliness, helplessness, etc.
fear of loss of love:	of punishment, rejection, desertion, earthquakes, thunderstorms, death, etc.
castration anxiety:	of operation, mutilation, doctor, dentist, illness, poverty, robbers, witches, ghosts, etc.

On the whole, these symbols are also interchangeable and, by themselves, an insufficient guide to diagnosis.

(iii) DEFENSE AGAINST ANXIETY, ABSENCE OF DEFENSE,
ITS ROLE WITHIN THE STRUCTURE

So far as a classification of the various fates of anxieties is concerned, the study of childhood cases is more productive than that of adult ones since the defensive moves against anxiety are more often incomplete, i.e., partly unsuccessful. This allows both sides to be visible on the conscious surface, on the one hand the manifest expression of the anxiety affect, on the other hand the ego's attempts to deal with the danger situations and their affective consequences by means of denial or avoidance, displacement or projection, repression, reaction formation, or any other available defense mechanism or defensive move, or a combination of several of them.

There is also the possibility for defense against anxiety to be lacking altogether, or to be wholly unsuccessful, in which case the affect reigns supreme in the form of *panic states* and full-blown *anxiety attacks*.[7] The occurrence of these is indicative that the child's ego has failed to acquire the important ability to reduce harmful panic anxiety to structurally useful signal anxiety, i.e., to the much smaller amount which is necessary to set defense in motion. Panics and anxiety attacks are not only extremely painful for the total personality of the child; they are, in fact, actually harmful for the ego which is swamped by them. Similar to true traumatic events, they temporarily put ego functioning out of action and thereby constitute a threat to the stability of the ego organization.

---

[7] For the clinician it is important to differentiate between such states and the common temper tantrums of childhood, which are manifestly similar but different as regards origin.

Classification of anxiety according to defense activity also provides clues for predicting the direction in which the child's further course is set: toward more or less normal adjustment; toward social or dissocial character formation; toward hysterical, or phobic, or obsessional or paranoid symptom formation or character development, etc.

2. The Delays or Failures in Development

It is well known by now that the developmental age of a child does not need to coincide with his chronological age and that fairly wide discrepancies in this respect are within the normal range. Children may be either fast or slow developers throughout. One also frequently sees that they change their rate of growing between one developmental phase and the succeeding one.

Nevertheless, a large number of children arrive in the clinic with the "referral symptoms" of unsatisfactory development, which, on clinical examination, may be found to range from the merest delay to the complete cessation of all forward movement on the lines of progress.

A child's failure to reach the expected level of growth may show up anywhere within the structure of his personality. It may concern the so-called milestones in the first year of life, i.e., the advances in motor development, the beginning of speech, etc. On the side of the drives it may concern a lagging behind on the prephallic libidinal and aggressive stages; in extreme instances, a failure to reach the phallic-oedipal level at all.

So far as the ego is concerned, the arrest may reveal itself in the quality of object relatedness, for example, in the persistence of anaclitic relationships at a time of life when object constancy is to be expected; or in the retardation of functions such as control of motility, reality testing, memory, learning capacity which remain below par; or in the defense organization which may remain at a primitive level of functioning via somatization, denial, projection, avoidance, etc., instead of advancing to repression, reaction formations, and sublimations.

The superego may be retarded either with respect to its autonomy, or its effectiveness, or with regard to the quality of its content, i.e., the crudeness of the internalized commands and prohibitions.

Developmental irregularities and failures of this kind confront the clinician with many problems, foremost among them the need to differentiate between the causes for them. Retardation of milestones in the first year of life raises the suspicion of *organic* damage (see Part I, 7). Delay in drive development either may be due to *constitutional* factors or may be determined *environmentally* by inadequate response from the parental objects. Ego retardation is frequently due to poor *endowment* but, as the study of many underprivileged children has revealed, equally often the consequence of lack of proper *environmental* stimulation. Arrested superego development may be part of general ego retardation (and share its causations); or it may be due to the lack of adequate objects in the child's *environment*; or to separations from them; or to *internal* failure to form relations to objects; or to the *qualities* of the parental personalities with whom the child identifies. Traumatic experiences may at any time endanger progress in any direction or, at worst, bring forward development to a complete standstill.

It remains as a task then to distinguish between these

developmental delays and failures and another type of damage to development which, though superficially similar, is different in kind. While the former refer to expected developmental steps not being taken, the latter represents the undoing of developmental achievements after they have been acquired and is due to regressions and inhibitions, i.e., based on conflict (see Part I, 2, neurotic symptomatology). Although the differential diagnosis here is important, and becomes all-important when the choice of therapy comes into question, confusion—especially between the effects of arrest and regression—is frequent.

There are few criteria to guide the clinician when, for example, he has to decide whether a boy has retreated from the phallic to the anal level (due to castration anxiety), or whether he has never reached the phallic stage; whether a child's superego has never proceeded beyond a primitive, crude level or whether it has become so at a later, more sophisticated stage of development, due to aggression turned inward and/or sexualization of its demands, etc. The most reliable hallmarks of neurosis are anxiety, guilt, and conflict, while in contrast to this the various types of developmental arrest may remain internally undisputed, especially in those cases where the arrest affects more than one sector of the personality. But this diagnostic indicator, too, cannot be trusted in all instances. Retarded children frequently react with anxiety and a semblance of guilt to the disapproval of their disappointed parents, while neurotic children are well able to deny conflict and guilt and thereby make them disappear from the manifest picture.

3. The School Failures

While all developmental failures are apt to arouse the parents' concern, usually they seek clinical advice most urgently when the child lags behind in age-adequate intellectual achievement and becomes a school failure. While the parents' concern exists regardless of the origin of the defect, in clinical examination it proves most important to distinguish between the different types of causation which can be subsumed under almost any of the different diagnostic categories discussed above.

Thus, learning difficulties, although they may be identical in their manifest appearance, may have to be allocated to any of the following categories:

  to *arrested development*, affecting either the person of the child as a whole, or the ego in general, or the ego's intellectual function in particular;
  to *undefended ego regression*, either global or in particular to the intellect;
  to *sexualization or aggressive symbolization*, either of the learning process as such, or of the particular subject to which the learning difficulty is attached;
  to *defense* against the symbolic dangers implied, especially by means of *inhibition* and ego restriction;
  to *symptom formation* of the neurotic types and its crippling effect on ego activity in general and sublimation in particular.

4. Failures in Social Adaptation

In this respect, as in the previous one, there is a marked discrepancy between the parents' concern which is easily alerted when a child fails to respond to moral standards, and their ignorance with regard to the causes which, either singly or combined, lead to the asocial, or dissocial, or delinquent or even criminal behavior which is produced.

On the basis of the reasoning which has gone before, failures in social adaptation can be seen in the following lights:

> as the logical outcome of adverse environmental circumstances such as neglect, lack of stability in object relations, separations and other traumatic events, undue parental pressure, failure of parental guidance, etc.;
>
> as the result of defects in the ego functions and the defense organization due to developmental arrests or neurotic regressions;
>
> as the result of economic alterations in the balance between id and ego;
>
> as the result of defects in the superego, caused by failures in object relatedness, identifications, internalizations, or by aggression used in its entirety against the external world instead of being in part at the disposal of the superego;
>
> as the result of faulty ego ideals, due to deviant parental models for identification.

In fact, causation of social failure is extremely varied in its nature, ranging, as it does, from the purely environmental to the near-psychotic. This has led to doubts among clinicians and some law teachers whether it is permissible at all to use the terms "dissociality" or "delinquency" as diagnostic labels, instead of speaking merely of dissocial or

delinquent actions committed by individuals who may belong to any number of diagnostic categories.[8]

5. Aches and Pains

What remains are the multiple aches and pains of childhood for which no organic cause can be found in physical
examination. They alarm the parents, and distress the
child. Incidentally, they also lead to innumerable absences
from school and, if massive, may constitute a serious threat
to formal education. They are also the most frequent reason for a child's medical referral to a child guidance clinic
or, in general, for a pediatrician's interest in the intricacies
of child psychology.

According to the metapsychological classification of
symptoms in Part I of this paper, the various aches and
pains of nonorganic origin can be traced back to three or
four of the categories enumerated there:

> to category 1, so far as they are the direct somatic ex-
> pression of mental processes;
> to category 2, so far as the affected body parts are sym-
> bolic of mental content and as such involved in men-
> tal conflict;
> to categories 3 or 4, so far as the affection of the body
> part is due to changes of cathexis, either qualitative or
> quantitative.

The diffuse aches and pains of childhood can be characterized as either psychosomatic, or hysterical, or hypo-

[8] See, for example, Joseph Goldstein of the Yale Law School
who opposes violently the use of "delinquency" as a meaningful
diagnostic term.

chondriacal. It hardly needs stressing that these different origins have a significant bearing on the evaluation of the presenting symptom, on the therapeutic approach to it, as well as on the prognosis with regard to its transience or permanency.

CONCLUSIONS

The Diagnostic Profile, as it is in use in the Hampstead Child-Therapy Clinic at present, is intended to draw the diagnostician's concentration away from the child's pathology and to return it instead to an assessment of his developmental status and the picture of his total personality. The present attempt at classifying the symptomatology of childhood may serve to amend and amplify this procedure by returning to the symptoms themselves a measure of diagnostic significance. If symptoms are viewed merely as manifest phenomena, dealing with them remains arid so far as analytic interest is concerned. If the clinician is alerted to see opening up behind these the whole range of possible derivations, causations, and developmental affiliations, the field becomes fascinating, and scrutinizing a child's symptomatology becomes a truly analytic task.

Besides, so far as work with children is concerned, diagnostic assessment is more than a mere intellectual exercise for the clinician. It is, in fact, the only true guide to the choice of therapeutic method.

As matters stand now, the form of treatment available for a disturbed child depends usually not on the specific category of his disorder but on the resources of the department or clinical facility to which he has been referred: institutional or foster parent provision if he is taken in care;

residential treatment if, legally, found out of control; weekly psychotherapy if referred to a child guidance clinic; family psychiatry, where this is the clinic's orientation; full-scale child analysis in a psychoanalytic clinic. It is only too frequent that the specific type of treatment applied is insufficiently matched with the specific type of disorder which should have been ascertained. Where this happens, children find themselves in institutions while they are in urgent need of individual, one-to-one relationships to develop their libidinal potentialities. Or they find themselves adopted, or in foster care, in spite of being far removed from the possibility of producing the child-to-parent attitudes which are an indispensable requirement of these situations. Or they receive analysis when education and guidance are needed; or guidance, when only analysis can solve their internal conflicts.

It is also futile to expect that any single method, whether superficial or deep, educational or therapeutic, will prove effective with disorders which are as different from each other as, for example, the neurotic compromise formations and the developmental arrests; or, so far as the learning failures are concerned, those caused by arrest, by undefended regression, and by inhibitions. Arrested children have to be treated educationally on their own mental level, an approach which fails disastrously where the therapeutic need is for the undoing of regressions or of lifting conflicts to consciousness, i.e., of freeing in the child an existing intellectual potentiality. Where the diagnostician remains on the phenomenological level and remains oblivious of the underlying fundamental differences, such therapeutic misapplications become inevitable.

The same plea for therapeutic differentiation (following

diagnostic differentiation) is justified where the child's fears and anxieties are concerned. It is as futile therapeutically to reassure a child in the throes of castration anxiety and guilt as it would be futile to approach separation anxiety at the symbiotic stage with analytic efforts. Fear of loss of love can be diminished by removal of external pressure, but only in those instances where its origin is due largely to environmental causes; not in others. Where fear of the id is present, as said before, parental leniency acts as an aggravating factor, not as a relieving one.

Where children commit delinquent acts, it is perhaps more obvious than with other disturbances that treatment has to be selected according to the cause either environmental, or developmental, or neurotic, or psychotic. No single type of therapy, however elaborate, or costly, or easily available, can possibly fit these widely different circumstances.

It is reasonable to expect that any step forward in the refinement of diagnostic assessment will, in the long run, lead to improvements in matching disorder and therapy in the children's field. The present paper is meant to represent a move in this direction.

APPENDIX

THE SYMPTOMATOLOGY OF CHILDHOOD

I. Symptomatology Proper

1. Symptoms resulting from the initial nondifferentiation between somatic and psychological processes=psychosomatic manifestations.

2. Symptoms resulting from compromise formations between id and ego=neurotic manifestations.

3. Symptoms resulting from the irruption of id derivatives into the ego=infantile psychosis, borderline states, delinquent states.

4. Symptoms resulting from changes in the libido economy or direction of cathexis=upsets in self and object valuation, depressive states, autism, emotional surrender.

5. Symptoms resulting from changes in the quality or direction of aggression=inhibition of functioning, accident proneness, self-injury, aggressive outbursts.

6. Symptoms resulting from undefended regressions= infantilisms, pseudodebility.

7. Symptoms resulting from organic causes:
   (a) from brain damage=delay of milestones, reduced quality of ego functioning, affective changes, etc.;
   (b) from sensory or anatomical handicaps=deviations in drive and ego development, multiple upsets of inner equilibrium.

II. Other Signs of Disturbance

1. The fears and anxieties (origin, content, defense, bearing on pathology).

2. The delays and failures in development (organic, constitutional, environmental, traumatic; differentiation from regression).

3. The school failures (developmental arrest, undefended ego regression, sexualization or aggressive symbolization and defense against it, neurotic inhibition, ego restriction, neurotic symptom formation).

4. Failures in social adaptation (environmental, developmental, economic, structural, neurotic, psychotic).

5. Aches and pains (psychosomatic, hysterical, hypochondriacal).

11

The Infantile Neurosis:
Genetic and Dynamic
Considerations
(1970)

I welcome my participation in this Symposium and expected that it would be a straightforward task to compare
the analysts' present ideas about the infantile neurosis with
those which were formulated half a century ago.

Nevertheless, when I began to approach the subject more
closely, I began to be doubtful about its legitimacy and
appropriateness. I felt that I was setting out to compare

Contribution to a weekend conference of English-speaking members of European Societies, organized by the British Psycho-Analytical Society and held on October 3 and 4, 1970, in London. The
theme of the conference was "Changing Concepts of Infantile
Neuroses and Their Effect on Theory and Technique." This paper
is here published for the first time.

two sets of propositions which had arisen on different grounds, fitted into different conceptions, and, in short, had not enough in common to be treated as if they were on a par.

THE CONCEPTION OF THE INFANTILE NEUROSIS AT THE TIME OF LITTLE HANS AND THE WOLF MAN

I assume that we take the case histories of Little Hans (1909) and the Wolf Man (1918) as outstanding examples of infantile neuroses, and the discussion of the processes involved in their disturbances as evidence of the then-reigning conceptions concerning this pathological manifestation.

When doing so, I suggest that we do not neglect in our evaluation one overridingly important difference between past and present. Psychoanalysis, at that period, was not concerned with infantile psychopathology as such. Interest and study were concentrated on the neuroses of adult life, their genesis, their dynamics, their relationship to normal character formation, their difference from the psychoses, etc. Infantile neurosis came within the focus of this interest only since it was one of the new findings, made by means of the new technique, that what is relevant for the formation of the adult disturbance are the underlying childhood experiences; i.e., that there is no adult neurosis, whether conversion hysteria, phobia, or obsessional neurosis, which does not have a neurosis in infantile life as its forerunner. Moreover, what was demonstrated in the case histories named above was the fact that both, the adult and the infantile disorder, shared the same motivation by conflict, the

same construction, the employment of the same mechanisms, and that their symptoms represented identical at
tempts at conflict solution, inadequate as the latter may be
if viewed from the aspect of reality adaptation. What I am
describing here is, of course, the well-known formula which
covers the formation of neuroses in general: conflict, followed by regression; regressive aims arousing anxiety; anxiety warded off by means of defense; conflict solution via
compromise; symptom formation.

It was assumed (though not proved at the time, since
there were no longitudinal studies) that the finding that
every adult neurosis is preceded by an infantile one is not
reversible; not every infantile neurosis is followed by neurotic illness in later life. This was taken to have a number
of implications such as the following:

that the infantile neurosis is *more frequent,* i.e., more
"normal," as an occurrence than its adult counterpart;

that many infantile neuroses are open to a *spontaneous
cure* which takes place at the point when the emotional
upheavals of early childhood are lightened by entry into
the latency period;

that it depends on the *experiences of adult* life whether
the childhood conflicts will be reactivated, i.e., whether a
new neurosis will be formed.

It is well known that the precipitating events for the
adult neurosis were seen in the conflicts between active and
passive sexual strivings; between heterosexuality and homosexuality; between object love and death wishes against the
same persons; between crude instinctual trends of all kinds
and opposing superego demands. The corresponding constellations for the infantile neurosis were found in the
stormy events of the phallic-oedipal period where conflicts

are likewise going on—conflicts between the positive and the negative oedipal attitudes; the masculine and feminine identifications; the ambivalences in the attitude to the parents; the castration wishes and castration fears of the male child; the conflicts between the different aims in life represented by the different structures within the personality (id, ego, superego). It was natural to assign the infantile neurosis, and especially its peak, to the phallic-oedipal period since full structuralization of the personality, full strength and independence of the superego, and accordingly full ability to develop conflicts resembling those of later life were not expected to exist before that time.

It would be a grave mistake, nevertheless, to assume that the infantile neurosis was ever taken to be the only representative of infantile psychopathology. It was merely that, at the time, it was the only one of great import for the analyst concerned with the adult neuroses. What remained outside this focal point were the intellectual defects, so far as they were not of a pseudonature, i.e., neurotic; the clinical pictures, then known under different terms, which are now labeled "autistic"; and the many failures of early physical or mental functioning which precede the oedipal period, are not due to conflict, and seemed of lesser relevance for the adult neurosis, even though their description was included in every analytic case history where they were treated as playing the role of preparatory or facilitating factors.

THE PRESENT SCENE

There is a world of difference between these studies of the past and the present scene. What we are pursuing at present are not evaluations undertaken from the viewpoint of any later mental disorder but an elaborate map of infantile mental difficulties as such, or, to express it more succinctly, an enumeration, description, and explanation of any inter- ference with optimal mental growth and development. On the basis of our knowledge of developmental phases, as es- tablished by reconstruction from adult analysis, by child analysis, by direct observation of infants and young chil- dren, we attempt to do this from birth onward, with the phallic-oedipal phase placed not at the lower but at the upper end of our investigation.

I contend that, due to these developmental considera- tions, we have stepped outside the realm of psychopathol- ogy in the usual sense of the term and have entered instead into a new area with new complexities: namely, into the study of early personality development. It appears almost as a by-product that, while doing so, we also assemble those developmental aspects which, in due course, will lend themselves to the production of conflicts and may even determine beforehand which among the available defense mechanisms the individual's ego will choose to employ and, accordingly, which forms of compromise and symptom for- mation will be open to him.

The Psychosomatic Reactions of Infancy

The distinction between personality background on the one hand and conflict-determined psychopathology on the other is illustrated by what follows here concerning the earliest difficulties of an infant in the areas of breathing, feeding, elimination, sleeping, skin sensitivity, etc. These difficulties, so far as they have no discernible organic cause, are physical as manifestations, and emotional as regards origin. They result on the one hand from interaction between inborn modes of functioning and the mother's handling of these potentialities, on the other hand from a kind of emotional infection emanating from her, i.e., from the infant's response to her moods, her anxieties, her preferences, and her avoidances. The affects engendered in the infant are discharged through the body; his physical experiences may find expression in his affective states. This easy access from mind to body and vice versa is known to be normal during the first year of life and becomes pathological only if it is maintained beyond this period after new pathways for discharge via thought, speech, and action have been opened up.

What is important to us here is that these early "psychosomatic" events make basic contributions to the building up of an individual's personality, especially by way of the pleasure-unpleasure, satisfaction-frustration experiences. It is an old finding that the satisfaction of early body needs opens up the way to object attachment and following this to the individual's general capacity for object relationships. In more recent times, observations and reconstructions concerning the first year of life have established that a lack of balance between pleasure and unpleasure, and especially a predominance of pain and frustration at this time, may prevent ego building and/or lead to lasting ego distortion and ego deviations from the norm; that a mother's failure to comfort her infant adequately may have lasting results for the individual's later general ability or inability to cope with even normal amounts of unpleasure, pain or anxiety.

What is primarily a personal attribute will then, secondarily, make its contribution to the child's psychopathology. That the form and strength of object attachments are decisive in the choice of neurosis is well known. Ego distortions may render the ego quite unfit to play its role in an infantile neurosis and may lead to the much more abnormal borderline states. A heightened intolerance for unpleasure leads almost inevitably to an exaggerated use of the ego's defense mechanisms and, consequently, to special severity of inhibitions and other neurotic manifestations.

There is, further, an even more direct manner in which the early psychosomatic events contribute to the later infantile neurosis. Whatever organ systems, physical functions or body parts (skin, intestinal tract, breathing, limbs, etc.) are involved in them, remain more vulnerable ever after than the rest of the child's physique and this creates the so-called "somatic compliance" of which later hysterical conversion will make use.

The Early Mother-Infant Relationship

The same difference between primary effect on personality development and secondary consequences for psychopathology are again met with in that area of the mother-infant relationship which is wholly psychological. The ingredients here are, on the mother's side, the manner in which she cathects the child's body and person, narcissistically or with object libido; with libido or aggression; positively or negatively; with or without significant changes and interruptions. On the infant's side, there is—subject to his inborn capacities—his reaction to her involvement, passive or active; pleasurable or painful; satisfied and comfortable or frustrated and demanding; loving, hating, ambivalent, etc. What arises on the basis of this highly complex mixture is the individual child's general attitude to himself and to the world around him.

It is an old psychoanalytic assumption that the experience of being well loved in infancy creates for all later life a feeling of security and self-confidence. We meet this again in the more modern literature under the terms of basic trust, self-regard and self-esteem. This determines on the one hand the balance between narcissism and object relatedness, on the other hand such personal characteristics as optimism or pessimism, courage or cowardice, outgoing or withdrawn attitudes. The relevance of these for psychopathology is obvious; they will be decisive for or against the occurrence of depression; for or against the choice of phobic mechanisms, etc. The constancy and strength of early object ties also facilitates internalizations and identifications, and these in turn enrich the personality on the one hand, and prepare the ground for conflict between the inner agencies, i.e., for neurosis, on the other hand.

The Component Instincts (Prephallic)

It may seem illogical to the listener or reader if the child's pleasure-pain, satisfaction-frustration experiences with his objects are viewed separately from those determined by orality and anality. This runs counter to our analytic experience that these two lines of development are intertwined and inseparable—that phase development depends for its normal unfolding on the presence of objects toward whom the component instincts can be directed; and vice versa, that object relations, even though shaped by the ego, derive their power and intensity from the libidinal and aggressive energies of the component instincts and reflect in their quality the dominant attributes of these early stages of drive development: greedy, demanding, dependent, incorporating during the dominance of the oral zone; clinging, possessive, torturing during the dominance of the anal one.

Nevertheless, the contributions toward both personality development and infantile neurosis made by the prephallic component instincts are different from those described previously, and this, I believe, merits a separate discussion. So far as personal attributes and character formation are concerned, they are, of course, well known; they enter into these either as residues of their original appearance or transformed into their opposites. But over and above this, they are of the greatest import for the formation of the infantile neurosis in two respects: (1) by preparing the way for regressions; and (2) by producing the base for neurotic compromise formations which can be considered to be the true forerunners of the infantile neurosis proper.

1. As regards regression: if we regard it as characteristic for the onset of a neurotic process that the individual's ego retreats from an ongoing conflict, danger or frustration to a previous, safer form of satisfaction, then the component instincts assume the special significance of being the agents which open up the opportunity for such returns. It is true that on the side of the ego, there also may exist tendencies to return to the past, based on inclinations to persevere, to maintain former modes of functioning and expression. But the latter, even where they are in evidence, fail to account for the powerful attraction which is exerted by the past, i.e., the force which propels an individual child backward, causes him to lose important developmental gains, and in-

volves him once more in the pursuit of primitive wish ful-
fillments which he had outgrown previously. Such happenings become plausible only if we think in terms of amounts
of instinctual energy which are latent on the early levels
and can be reactivated according to need, i.e., in terms of
fixation points to which regression takes place. It is implied
in this assumption that the energy amounts left behind are
those derived from the component instincts.

2. As regards symptom formation preceding the infantile
neurosis: even more to the point is the fact that it is the
area of the component instincts, i.e., the oral and anal
sexual trends and their frustrations, which produce early,
unmistakably neurotic symptoms. These may be hysterical,
phobic, or obsessional in nature, such as the affliction of
limbs; phobic reactions toward food intake and elimination, sleep or bath, loneliness; inhibitions of touch or motility; rigid insistence on regularity and absence of change;
obsessional intolerance of dirt, cruelty, etc. Overtly, these
manifestations are identical with the symptoms of a full-
blown infantile neurosis; but, on closer scrutiny, a number
of important differences between the two become apparent.

The *conflicts* on which this early symptomatology is
based are not between internal agencies, but represent in
the main clashes between an instinctual wish within the
child and a prohibiting or inhibiting influence in the external world, the only exceptions in this respect being those
caused by ambivalence, which arise as soon as the ego has
developed sufficiently to take notice of conflicting trends
and to be intolerant toward them. The *dangers* by which
the child's ego feels threatened at this time are attributable
not to fear of the superego, i.e., guilt, but to fear of the
object world, i.e., either of punishment or loss of love. *Re-*

gression from the forbidden wish of the moment to former
satisfactions may or may not take place; if it does, and if
no protest is raised by the environment, it is frequently
accepted as ego-syntonic by the child. The *symptoms* themselves are not interconnected and organized into syndromes,
as they will be later, but isolated and independent of each
other. Further, they are transitory, i.e., subject to changes
in the environment, changes in the ups and downs of object relations, and above all subject to developmental alterations in the importance and dominance of the instinctual
trends concerned. We may say that these early compromise
formations represent first attempts of the developing ego
to come to terms with frustration. But, compared with the
complexity of the later neuroses, this neurotic symptomatology is diffuse, unstable, and unorganized.[1]

The Phallic Phase

With the child's further progress through the next developmental stage, whatever psychopathology he will display assumes its final shape. What we expect from development
are decisive advances in structuralization, in every aspect
of ego and superego functioning and in the ego's ability to
hold its own. Where these moves occur, ongoing wishes
and fear of their disapproval by the object world lose their
role as direct pathogenic influences. Their place is taken by
regression when the wishes are frustrated, and this reactivation of developmentally earlier forms of satisfaction now
arouses internal disapproval, i.e., guilt. Accordingly, the
whole inner turmoil and the compromise solutions found

[1] A fuller description of this preparatory phase is given by Nagera
(1966).

for its relief are removed from external influence, become immovable through environmental changes, and may inhibit, distort or block further growth instead of profiting from progressive development.

Unlike its forerunners, what is now the infantile neurosis is no longer the ego's answer to the frustration of single trends, but is an elaborate attempt to deal with the whole upheaval caused by the action of conflicting drive derivatives; conflicting, exciting, pleasurable or painful affects; mutually exclusive attitudes toward objects—i.e., with the whole range of the oedipus complex and castration complex, set against the background of personal qualities and characteristics which have been established from infancy onward, and shaped by the fixation points which have been left behind during development.

Insight into these complex interactions between past and present, background and actuality, ego qualities and instinctual trends, conflicting identifications, opposite id tendencies, etc., are revealed to us in every analysis of an infantile neurosis. This does not mean that they are also easy to describe in their entirety. To enumerate and to integrate with each other whatever enters into the neurotic structure is no mean task, as shown, for example, in the final summing up of the Wolf Man case where we are presented by the author with a whole imposing array and sequence of contributing factors: a primal scene observation which leaves consequences for masculine or feminine identification; contributions from orality in the form of disturbances of food intake and fears of being devoured; urethral erotism in the service of identification with the father's masculinity; the experience of seduction which arouses early castration fears; contributions from the anal phase, on the one hand in the form of receptive-passive trends, on the other hand promoting aggressive strivings which predominate over anal erotism; earlier fears giving way to guilt which transforms sadism into masochism; passive-homosexual trends which succumb to the ego's fear of castration in the phallic stage. We are also shown how the comparatively simple anxiety hysteria with some features of conversion hysteria acquired an obsessional overlay, and how finally the whole upheaval subsides spontaneously with some residues left behind: inhibitions toward women which change to dependency toward them, some repetitive tendencies, a powerful "not entirely unconscious" inclination toward men, and an intolerance for narcissistic frustration which led to the reactivation of the infantile disorder in adult life.

Beyond the Infantile Neurosis

As mentioned before, not every child's psychopathology assumes the form of an infantile neurosis. The construction of the latter presupposes that various important developmental steps have been negotiated successfully and, as we know, this is not always the case. Due to constitutional defects, early deprivations, lack of suitable objects, wrong environmental handling, etc., the capacity for object relatedness may have remained inferior; identifications and internalizations may be weak; structuralization may be incomplete; the id-ego borders may be permeable; the ego itself may emerge from its early experiences as immature, deformed, distorted, etc. Where such developmental failures dominate the scene, the child will present clinical pictures on the border to much more severe pathology such as psychosis or mental deficiency; or he will remain arrested on the described lower level or disjointed neurotic symptom formation which corresponds to a preoedipal organization of the personality.

As analysts we hold a multiple view of the infantile neurosis. On the one hand, we regard it as belonging to the realm of psychopathology and realize that in its excessive forms it can be severe and crippling. On the other hand, we also know that it has a regular place in the childhood of many individuals whose future adaptation to life is successful, and that the conflicts underlying it are normal ones. Looked at from the developmental point of view, the infantile neurosis doubtless represents a positive sign of personality growth; a progression from primitive to more sophisticated reaction patterns and as such the consequence and, perhaps, the price which has to be paid for higher human development.

Technique

If, in the context of this paper, nothing has been said about the implications for therapy, the omission is intentional. The subject needs more space than could be given to it here, where I confine myself to one remark:

The psychoanalytic technique, including the technique of child analysis, was originally devised for, and has proved its worth in, the application to the neuroses proper, i.e., to the states of internal conflict where the ego needs assistance to widen its sphere of influence, and where this help can be provided via interpretation of the unconscious elements which are beyond its reach. In our times, the analysts' therapeutic ambition goes beyond the realm of conflict and the improvement of inadequate conflict solutions. It now embraces the basic faults, failures, defects, and deprivations, i.e., the whole range of adverse external and internal factors, and it aims at the correction of their consequences. Personally, I cannot help feeling that there are significant differences between the two therapeutic tasks and that every discussion of technique will need to take account of these.

12

Child Analysis as a
Subspecialty of Psychoanalysis
(1970)

The problematical subject of the status of child analysis and the question whether to consider it a subspecialty of psychoanalysis was introduced at the Twenty-Sixth International Psycho-Analytical Congress in Rome from the practical, administrative angle. It is the self-appointed task of the present convention to explore it further and to pursue its historical and scientific implications. Personally, I welcome this assignment, but before taking it up it is necessary to point to the much wider context in which the

Contribution to a symposium organized by the European Psycho-Analytic Federation on June 27 and 28, 1970, in Geneva, Switzerland. The theme of this symposium was "Child Analysis as a Subspecialty of Psychoanalysis." This paper is here published for the first time.

problem belongs and of which it is, at least in my own estimation, only one illustration among many others.

PSYCHOANALYSIS, REVOLUTIONARY OR CONSERVATIVE

It is well known that when psychoanalysis appeared on the scene three quarters of a century ago, it did so in a revolutionary spirit. As a discipline, it upset the then-ruling ideas of the scientific world and of the general public in a number of important respects. This was, in fact, one of the first times that the medical community was exhorted to take the mental troubles of their patients seriously, and to respond to them as compassionately as if they were physical ones, instead of dismissing as willful fabrication and pushing aside more or less contemptuously whatever suffering proved to have no organic cause. It was also the first time that the concept of an unconscious mind was taken out of the context of philosophical speculation and was shown to have practical implications for human behavior and for mental illness; that sexuality was seriously and openly discussed and assigned a dominant role in the production of neurotic disorders; that childhood impressions were shown to persist and to maintain a governing role in the adult's mental health, illness, and general functioning; that the early years of life, far from being a time of innocence, were seen to be governed by powerful instinctual strivings, clamoring for satisfaction; above all, that sexuality in its adult form was shown to have a prehistory from earliest childhood onward, with a number of component instincts and erotogenic zones leading to the final achievement of genitality.

Beyond these weighty aspects which represented the very essence of the new ideas, psychoanalysis also offended public opinion in some more minor practical ways. In spite of the distrust in which any kind of lay therapy was held by the medical corporations, Freud maintained his view that psychoanalysis could be practiced without a medical degree; in fact, that medical training was not essential as a preparation for the new profession. Nor was acceptance of psychoanalysis by the universities and its inclusion in their teaching programs considered vital, or even desirable. As a consequence, the training institutes of the analytic branch societies, once they came into being, remained outside of the accepted, conventional, academic organizations, as self-maintained structures, independent so far as selection of entrants, training programs, and qualifications for future membership were concerned.

Naturally, we do not expect the pioneering spirit of any movement to maintain itself over the years. It feeds on the very militancy which is needed to develop, emphasize, and protect new findings, and it subsides whenever acceptance, or even partial acceptance, for them has been gained. Moreover, the scarcity of rules and regulations within a movement which makes itself felt so pleasantly in the beginning becomes inadequate for the situation once the original small groups of adherents open their ranks and membership rises into the hundreds or even thousands. Newcomers are no longer welcomed with the same open arms; members, teachers, and students do not mix and participate as freely in scientific events as they did before. But, given that these changes are inevitable, it is still worthwhile to explore, in our special instance, to what extent they have altered the scene, and to what degree they influence the lives and actions of all of us who live and function within it.

It may be maintained, countering these arguments, that the revolutionary spirit in psychoanalysis is still in evidence, but this can be done only with one important qualification: that it still exists in the realm of scientific discussion and exploration; but it has been lost so far as administration and organization are concerned.

Psychoanalytic authors have been accused repeatedly of orthodoxy, i.e., of playing a scientific game of "follow the leader" in their publications. Whether or not this may have been true of certain historical periods in the development of the discipline, nothing can be further from the facts of the present situation. Only one glance at the psychoanalytic world literature of today is needed to convince the reader that there is among the contributors the liveliest discussion of all basic propositions, a discontent with the "classical," and a wish for the new, a yearning for extension to new fields of application, for new theoretical outlooks or, at least, new terminology. There is, in fact, no single item, either theoretical or technical, which has not come under attack in the literature by one author or another.

Free association, the keystone of analytic technique, has lost much of its ubiquitous use and has been accused, at least by one writer, of being not a path to unrestricted freedom of thought and expression, but an unwarranted authoritarian gesture, forcing the patient to communicate what he would prefer to keep to himself. *Dream interpretation* is now used by a minority of analysts and has yielded its role as the "royal road to the unconscious" to the interpretation of transference. *Transference* itself as a concept has changed its nature from a manifestation spontaneously arising in the patient's consciousness and behavior to one purposefully introduced into the situation by the analyst's interpretations. The role of *sexual trends* in the mental disorders is disappearing gradually behind that of their aggressive counterparts. The recall of *childhood* experiences in the analytic situation is considered by some analysts to be less important than the "here and now." On the metapsychological side, the economic aspect is falling into disrepute, while what is called structural now dominates the theoretical field. Above all, the introduction and redefinition of so many technical terms have brought with them new and so far unsolved difficulties for authors to understand each other's theories.

The situation on the side of organization and administration is the reverse. Whatever changes have occurred during the growth and development of our training institutions, they are not changes toward greater freedom or toward the introduction of new teaching methods. What has happened is the opposite. Selection of candidates for training has been narrowed down so far as personal and professional qualifications are concerned, in some countries to a degree which threatens the exclusion of the gifted or those from promising fields of application. The selection procedures themselves have hardened to what some applicants sometimes describe as unanalytic and insensitive. There is little or no change in the time allotted for study, although the material to be studied has increased beyond recognition. There is little or no room for experimentation or for pilot schemes. Admission of qualified students to full membership and participation in activities happens slowly, almost as if unwillingly. Admission of new local societies to the International Association happens according to compliance with regulations, rather than according to scientfic achievement of their members.

Thus, while there is revolution and almost anarchy in the field of theory and technique, there is rigidity, conservatism, and bureaucracy on the organizational side. The two may, in fact, not be unconnected. The more the scientific bonds between members and societies are falling apart in the absence of shared convictions and mutual understanding, the greater efforts are made, locally and internationally, to hold the membership together by means of increasing the number of rules and regulations. This is an unhappy state of affairs and creates an atmosphere which runs counter to the original psychoanalytic one. Child analysis, as I am going to show, falls a victim to it; but it is no more than one victim among many.

CHILD ANALYSIS: THE HISTORICAL ANGLE

There is no doubt that child analysis began as a subspecialty of psychoanalysis, in the period after the First World War when several such subspecialties were initiated. What was later known under the slogan of the "widening scope of psychoanalysis" were the attempts made from the 1920s onward to apply the therapeutic technique devised for adult neurotics to other ages or to other types of mental disorder. Siegfried Bernfeld did this for adolescents; August Aichhorn for young delinquents and criminals; Paul Federn for the psychoses; Hug-Hellmuth, Melanie Klein, myself, and the Bornsteins for children; Franz Alexander for the psychosomatic illnesses, etc. For most of these purposes, variations of technique were needed, in some instances permanent ones, in others no more than parameters, introduced temporarily for preparatory periods.

These extensions of psychoanalytic treatment not only benefited the new range of patients to whom they were applied. These analyses also yielded new knowledge which was carried back to and incorporated into the bulk of psychoanalytic theory, especially knowledge concerning the id-ego interactions, i.e., failures in the intactness of the ego borders (in adolescence, in the psychoses, etc.). But, in spite of the fact that such advances of insight occurred in all the new ventures, it would be a mistake to claim for child analysis no more than a place among them. Child analysis proved unique in one all-important respect: it was the only innovation which opened up the possibility of checking up on the correctness of reconstructions in adult analysis. This had previously not been feasible, apart from a few isolated instances where chance information extracted from outside informers about the patient's past had actually served to confirm an analyst's speculative constructions and interpretations.

Now, for the first time, with the direct application of psychoanalytic treatment to young children, what had been merely guessed at and inferred became a living, visible, and demonstrable reality. The libidinal strivings at various stages and the component instincts were seen in action. The oedipus complex was seen displayed toward the living parents in the external world as well as in ongoing fantasies and in the transference. The child's dependence on the figures in his environment was seen not merely from the distance of time but as an active agent in life and in the treatment situation. There was ample evidence to be had for primary process functioning, not only in dreams and symptom formation but in everyday behavior. What had appeared in reconstruction as single traumatic events revealed itself in child analysis as a sequence of such upsets, telescoped by recollection into cover memories.

I think that there was every justification to expect that all analysts of adults not only would be highly interested in these findings, but that they would also be eager to share the experience of having direct analytic contact with children of all ages, and to compare what emerges in child analysis with their reconstructions—in short, to undergo a training in child analysis, additional to the training for adults which they had received, and to apply it, at least in a number of selected cases.

Surprisingly enough, this development failed to occur, in spite of its being the only logical consequence of the situation. The analysts of adults remained more or less aloof from child analysis, almost as if it were an inferior type of professional occupation. The reasons offered for this attitude were manifold: that child patients were more difficult to obtain than adult ones; that their commitments to school, homework, etc., made their regular, five times weekly attendance impracticable; that the need to be accompanied made undue demands on the parents' time and patience; that the necessary attention to the parents was too time-consuming for the analyst; that the technique was difficult to master and, besides, lacked the decisive technical prescriptions which govern adult analysis and keep its practitioner on a straight and narrow path.

To those of us who already practiced child analysis much of this argumentation sounded like shallow excuses. It was difficult not to suspect that most analysts vastly preferred the childhood images which emerged from their interpretations to the real children in whom they remained uninterested.

However that may have been, child analysis did not have the triumphant career which we had envisaged for it. There were few local institutes which set up training in child analysis as part of their curriculum. Where this was offered, there were usually only a few candidates who availed themselves of the opportunity. Also, there was, almost everywhere, a scarcity of supervisors for child-analytic training. And, at best, training for child analysis remained scanty, not much more than an afterthought and a purely technical addition to the adult training.

CHILD ANALYSIS ON ITS OWN

No discipline can flourish under the circumstances described above.

For those of us who were committed to child analysis and concerned for its future, there was no alternative but to "go it alone" and to create over the years, regardless of official sanction or support, those conditions and institutions which we considered necessary and favorable for its growth. There was always the hope that, at some future date, the result of our efforts might be recognized and incorporated belatedly into the organizational framework.

If we survey the scene locally and internationally today, we find that child analysis has found a home in various places, apart from the grudging admittance given to it by the training institutes: in London in the Tavistock Clinic and the Hampstead Child-Therapy Course and Clinic; in Leyden and Amsterdam in the Training Course for Child Analysis; in Cleveland, Ohio, in the Training Course for

Child Therapists; in New York in the Child Development Center; in America generally in the Association for Child Psychoanalysis.

I speak in what follows from the vantage point of the experiences which I was able to gain in the Hampstead Child-Therapy Course and Clinic over more than twenty years.

So far as *training* was concerned, our isolation from an official institute forced us into a situation which seemed frightening and bewildering at first but proved beneficial in the long run. As mentioned before, the *technique* of child analysis had always been taught as an addition to the technique for adults, after the latter had been mastered, and more or less as a variation and modification of it. Since our training was confined to the area of childhood, we were faced with the task of developing and teaching our students an independent technique, not adapted from any existing one, but adapted directly to the needs and capacities of the child's immature personality at its various stages of development. Instead of being guided by the idea that a valid technique of child analysis needs to be as identical as possible with that for adults—an ambition which exists in various places—we were ready to admit that it needed to be different so far as children are different from their elders.

Our students, with only their own personal analysis as a model of procedure for adults, had, if anything, less than the average analyst's difficulty to accept a technique in which free association is nonexistent; in which transference is shared with the parents; in which there is a minimum of insight on the patients' part, coupled with a maximum of resistance; where the patient's treatment alliance is unstable and precarious and needs parental assistance in times of stress; where action takes the place of verbalization; and where the analyst's attention cannot be concentrated on the patient exclusively but needs to be extended to his environment. Our students also were less surprised than the average analyst that, despite all these aggravating differences in the working conditions, we nevertheless expected the aims of therapy to be in line with the known ones, i.e., to include the undoing of repressions, regressions, and inadequate conflict solutions; to increase the sphere of ego control; and, added to this, as an aim exclusive to child analysis: to free developmental forces from inhibitions and restrictions and enable them once more to play their part in the child's further growth.

We had less difficulty, of course, with the *theoretical* training where we could lean heavily on the traditions handed down in the official training programs of the institutes, at least so far as the literature on the historical development and the theory of psychoanalysis is concerned. Nevertheless, in these respects, too, some shift was needed in the weight and extent of the material. The child analyst needs to know enough of the psychoses of adult life to compare them with what is called childhood psychosis and to recognize as indicators of a psychotic substructure those outcrops from the unconscious which can arise in the context of any child's infantile neurosis; but he may need less in this respect than the analyst of adults. He needs to know everything about the adult neuroses, perversions, delinquencies, etc., of which the childhood disorders he is treating are the forerunners. His familiarity with the childhood disorders themselves should extend far beyond the scope of the infantile neurosis proper to the defects and failures of development and should include a skill in differential diagnosis. For the latter, in turn, solid knowledge of child development is needed since without it grave mistakes may be made in assessing what is pathologcal and what has to be included among the innumerable variations of a more or less hypothetical norm.

Obviously, an exacting program of this kind, added to the traditional personal analysis and supervision of clinical work, cannot be fulfilled in any *part-time* training, and this turned out to be another respect in which freedom to act independently proved of benefit. There was no reason for us to emulate the habits of either weekend or evening training which had been forced on the analysts by the harsh conditions of the pioneering period and carried without alteration into environmental circumstances which were different and much more fortuitous in every respect. Four years and a full-time commitment turned out to be a bare minimum for our purposes.

Again, I speak only for myself and for my colleagues in the Hampstead Course and Clinic, when I say that we see both the advantages and the disadvantages of independence. By rights, our students and graduates should be able to continue from child analysis to adult analysis, a widening of their experience which is denied to them under the circumstances. Furthermore, the careful theoretical training which they receive, added to the experience which they acquire in clinical psychoanalytic work, leads to abilities which should be at the disposal of the analytic communities at large instead of being confined to a small circle of workers who are looked on as "outsiders."

Nevertheless, for the reasons outlined previously, neither the local societies nor the International Psycho-Analytical

Association have any room for *experiments* in training or *pilot schemes* of any kind. So far the only exception in this respect is the Dutch Society. It is their courageous action of incorporating the Leyden Training Course which served to open up the discussion of the whole complex topic.

FUTURE OUTLOOKS

We are presented, thus, with an anomaly within the psychoanalytic scene. There are large numbers of analysts who have never met analytic childhood material except in reconstruction. Conversely, there is by now a considerable number of elaborately trained child analysts of whom merely a fraction are gaining admission for further adult training, and these, at least in England, without even receiving due credit for their previous studies. If we look at psychoanalysis from the point of view that it should embrace all ages and stages of human development, both trainings are sadly *incomplete* and the whole state of affairs is a highly unsatisfactory one which augurs badly for the future.

The conveners of this conference have been emphatic in their request that those who participate in discussion should restrict themselves to the scientific aspects of the problem and reserve its practical solution for the deliberations of the forthcoming Twenty-Seventh International Congress. I must confess that, for once, I find it almost impossible not to overstep my assignment. Those of us who either originated child analysis, or served it for long periods of time, cannot but feel themselves competent to offer guidance and advice on the administrative issues which may shape its future.

I see the problems waiting for solution as follows:

There is the question whether our international body will take the present developments as given and, to eliminate the worst incongruities, will advise the local societies to follow the example of the Dutch and *offer some form of recognition* and acceptance to those who are child analysts only, while leaving all else as it is at present.

There is also the possibility that they will go further and take a decisive stand on the view that no analyst can consider himself *fully trained* so long as his clinical experience and technical skill are confined to any one age or stage of development; that all child analysts should be encouraged to seek experience with adults, while all analysts of adults should analyze at least a sample number of children; that lack of such opportunity, or failure to make use of it, deprives an analyst of the privilege to be equally knowledgeable about past, present, and future of his patients.

If the latter view is taken seriously at all, it means that a *multiple training* for children, adolescents, adults, the older ages, will become the rule instead of being the exception, just as it is the rule now to be trained for the analysis of a variety of mental disorders. Naturally, there will always be individual analysts who show greater aptitude for dealing with one specific age, or type of personality, or type of illness than with others, and they will wish to specialize in their chosen field. But to me it seems important that any *specialization* in psychoanalysis should happen after training, and even after a period of gaining all-around experience, and should not precede these. After all, the same basic clinical and theoretical training is needed for all later eventualities, and the appropriate additions needed can be given whenever such a special area of work is entered, temporarily during training, or more permanently at a later date.

There are many advantages to such a new regime, apart from and beyond widening the analyst's general outlook. Where specialization has taken place, either in childhood or in adulthood disorders, analysts will be entirely free to *transfer* again from one field to another, according to the professional opportunities which are available, according to their own changing preferences, according to age, etc. They will not be tied to a limited section of psychoanalysis as they are now.

I do not disregard the added difficulties for our *selection procedures* which are implied in such changes. There will be applicants who meet the requirements for work with children much more obviously than those for work with adults, and vice versa. I think our selection committees will have to resign themselves to this so long as the personal obstacles do not go far enough to preclude a basic training in both directions. Incidentally, candidates who are too set in their personalities will loosen up in child-analytic work, while those who are more immature will ripen in their contact with adult patients.

Obviously, also, for the two types of work different previous professional experience is needed, whether in education, psychology, sociology, medicine or psychiatry, and at least some familiarity with all these fields has to be looked for to make a basic psychoanalytic training practicable.

CONCLUSION

I think we have good reasons to look hopefully toward the discussions which are planned for the Vienna Congress.

The problems of the status of child analysis may stir up wider issues which concern the status of psychoanalytic training in general. Perhaps the Congress, or the relevant Committee at the Congress, will arrive at the conclusion that our training programs, as they exist now, need to become more elaborate, more comprehensive, with more time given to them; and that many of the restrictions by which they are now hedged in are conservative relics of the past, in need of a revolutionary overhaul.

Part II

13

Residential vs. Foster Care
(1967 [1966])

<hr>

When I was invited to comment on the papers and the discussion of the first day of this workshop, I took it that I would not be expected to summarize the various points that were made, but, rather, to give my subjective impressions. I hope that you expect nothing else of me.

When the members of the workshop were introduced, my first impression was that there were as many important workers with children present as there are important aspects

Presented at a conference jointly sponsored by the Child Study Center of Yale University and the Children's Bureau, held in April, 1966, in New Haven, Conn.

The paper presented a summary of the first day's reports given by Sibylle Escalona, Eleanor Pavenstedt, Harriet Tynes, Joseph Gavrin, Bettye Caldwell, and Halbert Robinson.

First published in *On Rearing Infants and Young Children in Institutions,* ed. Helen L. Witmer. Washington: U.S. Department of Health, Education, and Welfare, Children's Bureau Research Reports, No. 1, 1967, pp. 47-55.

of a child's personality. The question then arose as to the aim of this workshop. Is it possible to combine in one mind the various experiences that the many people here have gained from their personal work with children? For only if we can make a constructive summary of this information can we hope for a constructive application of our knowledge.

I think one of the faults in the children's field is that training is so specialized. We have a division between medical knowledge, educational knowledge, and psychological knowledge. Then there is a further division within psychological knowledge: between knowledge about the emotional self and knowledge about the intellect. Since all these types of knowledge concern one and the same child, they should be combined somewhere in one mind.

Moreover, there is a division along age lines. Usually, people who work with elementary school children do not work with high school children. For this reason the knowledge about one phase of life is rarely seen as it ought to be seen, namely, as a step in preparation for the next phase, and not as applied to only one particular portion of a child's life.

Again, there is a division between teaching and upbringing, and teachers often know very little about the activities of those concerned with the actual rearing of children, and vice versa.

We cannot blame the workers in the different research fields for this state of affairs. We must blame our training schemes, as well as the fact that there is no free movement of professional workers between the various sections. I know that this state of affairs has improved a little in recent years. There are some nurses who know something about healthy children. There are even some teachers who have visited hospitals. However, there are very few teachers of older children who have ever worked with infants, and there are very few people who are equally familiar with the care of a child's body and a child's mind. In planning for future improvements I think that such an interchange within work for children is almost essential. Without that, many of our plans wll not materialize. This change, however, cannot come about without decisive changes in the training of personnel.

Even more serious is the fact that the division between theory and practice is widespread. There are many people who work on the theory of child development, and there are many others who work practically with children. But not enough theorists have the opportunity to apply their theories, and too few practitioners are taught developmental theory while they work directly with children.

In this respect, I have been especially fortunate all my life. From the very beginning, I was able to move back and forth between practice and theory. I started out as an elementary school teacher. I changed from that to the field of analysis and child analysis. From then on, I moved constantly back and forth, from the theoretical study of these problems to their practical application. I agree that one has to have special luck to do this, and that most people do not have this. Personally, I have to be grateful to a number of persons and institutions for giving me that opportunity.

When I was still very young in my psychoanalytic studies but had learned enough to apply at least some of the knowledge, I was asked by the city of Vienna to make that knowledge available to teachers of nursery schools and elementary schools. I was given the opportunity to work with small groups of teachers, to discuss their practical problems with them in easy, theoretical terms. This proved to be useful to them and was immensely useful to me (see Anna Freud, 1930).

When I had learned a bit more about psychoanalytic theory, an American friend gave me and some colleagues the opportunity to begin an experimental nursery for children between one and two years of age. (It was experimental because at that time group care for children of that age was unheard of.) The children we worked with were the most underprivileged children that could be found in Vienna. For such children, to begin education and therapy at three is much too late. Our entrance requirement was ability to walk—not necessarily to walk well, but to be able to get from one place to another, to have a certain amount of free movement. This was an excellent opportunity for us to learn and to test out some of our theoretical ideas in an active plan of day care.

The next opportunity of that kind was provided, not by a person or by an institution, but by an emergency, the emergency being World War II. This, of course, was a marvelous opportunity, for if anybody wanted to try out a scheme of residential care of children, what better excuse for it was there than war conditions, when the children had to be separated from their parents for reasons of safety. These war conditions, combined with the generosity of an American charity, the Foster Parents' Plan for War Children, made it possible for me and some colleagues to try out a residential scheme for a period of five years. We learned intensively and extensively how to care for eighty resident children from birth to the age of five (see Dorothy Burlingham and Anna Freud, 1942, 1944).

My next venture in putting theory into practice was the

Hampstead Clinic, in which I continue to work. This introduced me again to the whole range of problems: of day care in nurseries for normal children and for handicapped (that is, blind) children; of well baby clinics and of outpatient treatment of problem children, mostly neurotic. This had two advantages for me personally. It provided an opportunity to maintain a close connection between theory and practice, to check constantly on theoretical ideas by practical application, and to widen practical handling and practical measures with the growth of theoretical knowledge. It also had another advantage. Having worked in day care, in residential care, and in outpatient care, I had all the vested interests combined inside myself. If they conflicted with each other, they conflicted in me, and I could argue them out with myself without hurting anybody's feelings when finding that one or the other was better or worse than the rest.

This is enough of an introduction about my personal luck. Now to the point of the discussion today. Naturally, I bring my own experiences to bear on what has been said.

A point was made this morning that hostile feelings sometimes play a part in creating institutions for children. I would like to add that very often one has the impression that affectionate feelings also are at work. I would make the point that it should not be feelings of any kind that determine the type of care to be given to children.

I remember that a long time ago—it may well be forty or forty-five years—when I first faced an audience to whom I was supposed to talk about the care of children, I expressed astonishment that in this field we proceed to action without inquiring into the quality of the material with which we deal. I wondered then, and I still wonder, what our position would be if we entered, for instance, the field of metal work or work with wood or leather merely on the basis of feelings—because we liked it or because we disliked it or because we wanted to alter its shape. We would not get very far.

Work with metal, and ideas about what can be constructed from it, are based on the quality of this particular material. Whatever plans are made for it are made on the basis of the knowledge of these qualities—whether you can bend it, heat it, etc.

But it has not been so with work with children. This has been determined by extraneous factors—by feelings about them, financial possibilities, social opportunities, religious motives, or the very personal motives of a child worker. I think that many of the unexpected outcomes and many failures have been simply due to the fact that the handling of children has not been based on knowledge of their nature.

Things have changed, of course, in the last thirty or forty years. But I think very seldom has a conference expressed as clearly as this one that we should start with the developmental needs of childen, and that plans for children should be based on detailed knowledge about their needs and the possibility of meeting those needs. That seems to me the outstanding thing about this conference.

We have heard two impressive descriptions of children's needs, one applying to the first two years of life and the other to the period from two and a half to five. When we deal with the first years of life, we are in a favorable position, since for that age it is possible to define developmental needs in fairly global and fairly simple terms. A child's needs, one might say, are simpler the younger the child is. Still, as we heard from Escalona, they are complicated enough. Escalona divided them into primary needs and those that are subordinate to primary needs. If we leave out this distinction for the moment (for I would call some primary that she listed as subordinate), I think we could summarize them as the emotional needs of the child.

Escalona described as important for a child's development that he be of emotional importance to his caretaker, that he have adequate stimulation, that the processes of stimulation include give-and-take between child and caretaker, that there be continuity in care (continuity and stimulation at the same time), and that the environment be what we might roughly call normal.

When I said that at this time of life a child's needs are simple, I was exaggerating. Complications are introduced into the scheme by the fact that the needs interact with each other. Among the most important things we have learned in the last twenty or thirty years is the fact that the emotional growth of a child cannot be separated from his intellectual growth. On the one hand, we have learned that a child's intellect is stimulated from the emotional side, that it reacts differently in close contact with an important love object in his life. On the other hand, we have learned that this relationship to the caretaking adult, to the parent, is shaped above all by the growth of the ego function in the child. The first primitive relationship alters gradually to a mutuality with the loved object—recognition of the mother's or father's qualities and needs, concern for them, and loyalty to them. This could not come about if functions in the child which we ascribe to the other side of the child's life, namely, the ego functions, had not ripened, matured, developed at the same time. Even though, for theoretical purposes, we have to divide the streams of emotional and ego development from each other, we also have to have the ability to see them in interaction and to see their mutual dependence on each other.

Continuity of the loved caretaker is of course necessary for emotional development, for the development of mutuality between mother and child, and for stimulation. If any of these is interrupted in a significant way, the child loses his gains in growth and, as we call it, regresses. To make matters more complicated, all these needs of the child have to be satisfied in a suitable environment, a so-called normal environment. This again shows the dependence of the various factors on each other.

We have heard Pavenstedt's excellent description of what happens at the next stages. She has given this description by reviewing very briefly all the aspects and activities, events and happenings in a child's life. If one wanted to summarize it in technical terms, which Pavenstedt has rightly avoided doing, we would say that this is the time when the child goes through the whole sequence of drive development (sexual development and aggressive development) and, at the same time, goes through the two biggest complexes in his life, the oedipus complex (the relationship to father and mother) and the castration complex (the recognition of the difference between the sexes). This is also the time when the personality becomes structured, that is, divided inside. Pavenstedt expressed it by saying that the child ceases to be carefree. The child ceases to be a unified person and begins to develop conflicts within himself. If you sum up Pavenstedt's descriptions, you have the emergence of a structured, complicated, semi-adult personality out of the infantile being with whom we dealt in the first two years of life.

How can we express this in terms of the child's needs? You realize that what is needed from parents or their substitutes in this phase of the child's life is enormous, but is there any way in which we can compress it into one or two points? Perhaps I only take the meaning out of it when I say that what the child needs is the right setting within which he can experience all his ongoing concerns, problems, and conflicts, and that his need is for help in problem solving. What we call the good or helpful parent in these years is the parent who can give the child unobtrusive but steady assistance in overcoming one anxiety after another, one crisis after another, one conflict after another, so that he is not arrested at any stage of development but can pass on to the next—sometimes only from one problem to the next, and from one conflict to the next. But, after all, that is life.

After hearing these two expositions of children's needs, we have to ask ourselves in which setting (family care, day care, foster home, residential home) which needs are fulfilled, and in which are they left unfulfilled? Before we arrive at an answer I have to mention a point that has been very helpfully brought into the discussion and that complicates the question.

It seems that we have been discussing two problems at the same time, the problem of the normal child, his developmental needs and their fulfillment, and the problem of the deprived or rejected child and the attempts to fulfill his needs. Sometimes we have talked about the one, and sometimes we have talked about the other. It seems to me that the way out of this confusion is not to give preference, in the first instance, to any one type of child but to consider the various types of care and weigh them against the certainty of children's needs.

As Escalona has pointed out, the well-functioning family is capable of meeting all the needs of the child, at least those that we have acknowledged:

1. The need for continuity. This need is met if the family is a stable one and stays together.

2. The need for stimulation. This is met if the family is oriented in that direction and knowledgeable enough to give the child what he needs, or intuitive enough to respond to the child's demand in that respect.

3. The need for mutuality between mother and child. The normal mother gains as much pleasure from the interchange as the child does.

4. The need for affection. This is met as a matter of course, for the child is an important member in such a family.

5. The need for help in working out the complexes, conflicts, and problems of development. Good parents are able to give the child help in this respect.

This is an idealized picture of a well-functioning family, of course. A family becomes less good in our eyes if one or the other of these conditions is not fulfilled. If a family fulfills none of these needs of the child, we have no reason to give preference to family care over any other kind of child care. If a child is not loved—and this does happen—we certainly feel that he should be removed from the family.

If a child is not an important member in his family, however, we become alarmed. In our Clinic, for example, we become suspicious when, in the referral of a young child, we deal with a mother who cannot give us any information about when the child smiled first, walked first, spoke his first words, when he first developed his various abilities. If the mother really does not remember, we feel the child cannot have been very important to her at that time. We see other mothers who have every activity of their children engraved on their memory. Sometimes, to our surprise, we see couples where it is the father who remembers and the mother who does not. In any event, this is only one of the hints as to the role a child plays in his family. Certainly, it is rare enough that parents fulfill all the needs of a child, even though the possibility is there.

A child is seldom as important to his parents as the parents are important to him, or as the child would like to be. This is so because, in the child's early years, the parents have many other involvements and concerns, whereas the child at that time has only his parents as his concern. This is very unfair, but this is how it is.

If, with this point of view in mind, we review the whole range of possible child care facilities, we come to the foster family next. An indictment made today of foster families was that they promise to fulfill what they often cannot fulfill: that is, the child's need for continuity. There may be affection, there may be stimulation, there may be mutuality for a while, but there is not the tie between the foster parents and the child that guarantees this continuity. It does not seem reasonable to expect full parental involvement from foster parents without guaranteeing them full parental possession. This is a reason for ending the legal rights of parents who do not fulfill their obligations. By taking away their legal rights we make it possible for others to take over in the role of parents.

The foster parent, then, is not a real parent. If we go down the list of children's needs, we see that the chance of their being unfulfilled, or of some of them being unfulfilled, is much greater in a foster family than in a natural family.

Another question arises here. We do not know whether the lack of fulfillment of one need has repercussions on the others. What happens in this respect when continuity of care is not provided or when affection is missing? These are questions to explore further.

I think we have no doubt (and the principle has been confirmed by Caldwell's description) that day care has the greatest chance of meeting the child's need for stimulation. What we usually do not demand from day care is the fulfillment of children's emotional needs, since these can be taken care of at home. The relationship of a child to a teacher or the caretaking person in day care is of a different nature from his tie to his parents. He demands something different and receives something different from each of them. What he receives has to be of a quality which renders the stimulation effective. Otherwise, day care itself will not be effective. In day care, continuity is not as important as in the other child care arrangements. This should make us suspect that the need for continuity is more closely linked with emotional needs than with the need for stimulation—which is perhaps obvious.

In the difficult area of residential care—one of our main concerns in this meeting—I am glad that we have the benefit of the excellent descriptions of actual programs. In Gavrin's account there is a clear description of the battle for continuity that goes on in residential care. Naturally, we can give stimulation in residential care, and we have heard how one can give affection to babies in residential care. One can give it also to older children. One can carry over from day care to residential care most of the other advantages that Caldwell described. But what about continuity, what about the emotional development of the children?

I was much interested in the point made by Gavrin that one can try to attach the children to the idea of the house, the institution, and that this can perhaps substitute in part for personal attachments, which we would so much want to be continuous without having the power to make them continuous. This suggestion, however, is not true for children of all ages. I know that it is true for older children. I know that an older child will sometimes quite deliberately replace the loyalty to a person by loyalty to a house, a home, but young children cannot develop this sort of attachment.

Whether rightly or wrongly, a comparison with domestic animals comes to mind here. We know that cats are attached to houses and dogs are attached to persons. To change this around—to attach a dog to a house and a cat to a person—seems to be impossible. It is similar with children. A toddler is attached only to persons. A six-year-old may be attached to a house as well as to a person. This is very much a question of age. In residential institutions we try to make such events as leaving meaningful for the child, but I think this works better for the adults who do it than for the children. For a young child to leave the only people to whom he is attached is a terrible experience, however it is done. Parting ceremonies work very much as funeral ceremonies do. They are attempts to put feelings into a prescribed form and to relieve consciences. Even so the loss remains. And the loss to a child can, of course, be tremendous.

The question of continuity in a residential institution is twofold. On the one hand, there is the change of staff. The younger the staff, the more frequent are the changes; and the older the staff, the less fit and apt are they to deal with young children. Of course it helps, as Gavrin said, if certain key people remain constant and influence the in-coming staff. But this will not comfort a two-year-old or a three-year-old, only the older children.

On the other hand, continuity is also broken by outside powers working on the institution. Children are snatched away and put into other homes for reasons that have nothing to do with their development. This brings about breaks and separations which the institution is impotent to combat and which are tragedies for the children. So whenever residential care is proposed, these points have to be kept very carefully in mind.

Overall, then, I think the order of preference is care by the child's own family, foster family care, residential care—with day care somewhere in between.

In this comparison between various forms of care there is an additional reason why family care comes out best. I have already pointed out that this form of care makes it possible to provide for all the needs we have listed. But even if a given family does not do this wholly adequately, such care seems preferable because it is easier to complement a family by providing day care than it is to complement day care or some other form of foster care by giving a child the needed affection and personal relationships from some other source. If this is the case, I can only repeat what has been said before: we should explore carefully how many of the homeless children who are now living either in foster families or in institutions are there of necessity. I would like to remind you of the difference between alterable and unalterable conditions that Escalona introduced into the discussion.

Do the authorities really do everything in their power to promote family care—to enhance it, to make it financially possible? Are not many children deserted, for example, by their unmarried mothers, children who could be kept at home if the mothers received adequate financial support? Couldn't many children be with their families or relatives if support were forthcoming? This would be very much cheaper than keeping the child in an institution or in some other form of care, and better for the child.

If we were fully convinced of the superior advantage of family care, much effort would be concentrated on helping home life to fulfill children's needs. This help can take the form of financial support; it can take the form of advice and guidance; it can take the form of supplementation of home care by intensive day care. This, I believe, is the best use that can be made of day care. Day care should be geared to the lacks in family care; i.e., it should supplement family care. In this connection we should also note that deprived and underprivileged children are apt to need this supplemental care at an earlier age than do more privileged, middle-class children.

There is another type of child whose home life, I think, should be supplemented in all instances by advice and by day care. This is the handicapped child, whether mentally or bodily handicapped. In Hampstead we have studied intensively the situation of blind children and have found an intense need on the part of their mothers to be helped from the very beginning. Even if you take the point of view that parents are equipped through their personal relationship with the child to fulfill his needs, I am of the opinion that this does not apply when a child's needs are complicated by physical or mental handicaps. In all these instances, supplementary care is very necessary and can in many cases prevent a breakdown of home care.

I would note, too, that foster family care should be helped in many ways before it is given up as unsatisfactory. One way of doing this would be to raise it to the status of a profession. Why should it not be an honorable profession to raise children who are not one's own? This is a profession that needs knowledge, time, personal application, devotion. Why should it be the only profession that is not adequately rewarded? In many countries (and I think the United States is one of them) the social status of a profession is determined to a large degree by what one can earn in it. So I think that if one could earn an adequate salary by being a good foster parent, the status of the profession would not be so different from that of being a good doctor or a good teacher or a good lawyer or a good psychiatrist. I do not see the difference.

I believe this would make an enormous difference, not only in the quality of foster care, but also in its continuity. At present we count on foster care being paid for by something that foster parents do not get, namely, the feeling that they possess the child. Since they do not possess him, they should have some other compensation for all the work they put into the task.

Further, it is even more important for foster family care than for home care to be supplemented by good day care. To devise help for residential care is much more difficult.

We know that residential care is greatly aided by the nursery school it provides. This helps with the stimulation of the children. Residential care is also very much helped by choosing the right staff and by giving the staff satisfaction apart from direct contact with children. We know, too, that residential care is very necessary for certain types of children, as a therapeutic environment. But whether we can ever produce continuity in residential care, and how this will influence the other factors, are still open questions.

One last point. Provence's plan to make comparative studies between the different types of possible child care is, of course, an excellent one. To my mind, it is especially excellent if we do not take the word "comparison" too literally. We cannot really compare results, since the children who go into these schemes are different children. The result is always determined only in part by the handling of the child; for the other part it is determined by what the child brings with him to the situation.

A comparison of this kind is immensely valuable, however, if we restrict it to another side of the matter. If instead of highlighting children we highlight problems of care, we can build up these different types of care with the definite intention of watching for the problems that arise and of understanding each problem as it arises. We will probably get three different sets of problems, which we can then compare.

14

Film Review

John, Seventeen Months: Nine Days in a Residential Nursery by James and Joyce Robertson (1969)

We owe James and Joyce Robertson a considerable debt for confronting us with happenings in the lives of young children which otherwise are brought to our notice only once removed through the verbal accounts of adult witnesses, or removed in time through their later revival and reconstruction in analytic therapy. The demonstrations *ad*

First published in *The Psychoanalytic Study of the Child*, 24: 138-143, 1969.

oculos offered by the Robertsons' films are, to my mind, "direct observation at its best."

These films have gained wide acclaim and have engaged their viewers' interest in a whole range of topics. There was *Laura*, aged two, doing her inadequate best to cope with the double experience of separation and hospitalization; *Sally*, aged twenty-one months, meeting bodily discomfort, medical interventions, and the strangeness of hospital life, supported by her mother's presence; *Tom*, the thalidomide victim, growing up painfully but courageously as the only cripple in the tumultuous world of normal nursery children; there were *Kate*, two years and five months, and *Jane*, seventeen months, in brief separation from their own homes, their distress handled and alleviated by an exceptional type of foster care.[1]

What was brought home to us in each instance was the impact of the external circumstances on the children's inner experience, as evidenced by their facial expressions, their motor responses, their outbursts of emotion, and, quite especially, the relationship between their general behavior and the length of duration of the stressful situation.

However, whatever lessons have been learned from these earlier productions, they have been far surpassed by the latest documentary, devoted to *John*, seventeen months, and his nine days' stay in a residential nursery. The "nine days" are emphasized with justification. We can never be reminded sufficiently that such a period of time, short by adult standards, may be long enough for a child under two to shatter his existing personality, to disrupt the ongoing

[1] See James Robertson (1952, 1958) and James and Joyce Robertson (1967, 1968, 1969).

course of development, and to do long-lasting harm to his normality.

Judged by the prevailing standards of knowledge of a young toddler's needs, no blame attaches to the parents for placing John as they did during the mother's unavoidable absence in the hospital for the confinement with her second child. Whether fathers can stand in for the mother in taking care of a seventeen-months-old for twenty-four hours a day is a question still under exploration. However that may be, John's father was prevented altogether from attempting this due to exacting professional demands. In the absence of supporting relatives, the parents took the family doctor's recommendation to place John in this institution with small groupings, sufficient staff, and an overall efficient, friendly, and nonpunitive atmosphere. They could feel certain that John would receive very adequate body care and that he would be kept safe during the brief interval until his mother could receive him back.

Nevertheless, in the prevailing standards of knowledge it tends to be overlooked that even toddlers, and quite especially toddlers, "do not live by bread alone." Their needs for nourishment, cleanliness, comfort, and security are inextricably bound up with the feelings that tie them to their mothers, who carry out the function of ministering simultaneously to both sides of their natures, the material as well as the libidinal requirements. Only while this happens will the child be sufficiently at peace for internal growth and for increasing interest in and adaptation to the external world.

The film sequences on Kate and Jane left us no doubt that it is difficult for any fostering agency to assume the role of the familiar love object in a child's life. Young children under the impact of emotional loss and deprivation make demands which are excessive by any ordinary standards. We witnessed that it was only by not sparing herself and by being fully available to respond to the mothering needs of her foster children that Joyce Robertson enabled them to come through the separations without being overwhelmed and to return unharmed to their mothers. We can feel convinced that under the conditions of communal life, as in a residential institution, there is not the slightest chance to meet the separated child's requests in terms of time, effort, patience, and exclusive attention.

Moreover, the change from family life to communal life is never advantageous at this age. A cherished only child such as John is unprepared for the aggressive atmosphere of an institutional toddler group. He is not versed in the reigning modes of attack and defense; he has not learned to grab what he wants; nor is he used to having some precious possession unexpectedly snatched from his grasp. The concept of sharing, so essential in group life, is still far removed from his understanding.

Consequently, instead of profiting from the availability of potential playmates, John can only experience the presence of the other children as a constant threat from which he would like to withdraw to a protecting adult. While, initially, his retreat and search is directed toward a "familiar" face, the constant change of nannies soon makes him more promiscuous, i.e., less discriminating: any adult will serve the purpose so long as she pays attention (such as the nanny who bathes him). However, any individual attention received is either too impersonal in nature of too fleeting in duration to counteract John's growing bewilderment, frustration, and withdrawal into himself.

Nor do the father's visits help much to improve the situation. His coming and going, which are unrelated to the child's needs and wholly beyond his control, seem to aggravate rather than to decrease tension.

While following the film sequences, we cannot help but think in terms of two concepts which played an important part in Ernst Kris's studies of the behavior of young children; in the first instance, their *regression rate* (1950); in the second instance, the connection between *strain and trauma* (1956).

As regards *regression*, I believe that Ernst Kris would have assessed John's reactions as fairly normal and predictable. Far from losing his developmental gains indiscriminately, he proceeds on a retrograde course gradually. From constructive play (according to description, a child "who amused himself") he returns to cuddly toys, from there to aimless wandering and manipulating. From babbling words he regresses to toneless whining and whimpering; from interest in his surroundings, to thumb sucking. Whether the disruption of bodily functions (vomiting, diarrhea, food refusal) should be classed under the same heading is an open question.

As regards *trauma*, we have to guard here against using the term in the most ordinary sense. What has happened to John is not, according to the common definition of trauma, "a sudden overwhelming experience with an influx of stimuli by which his ego is temporarily (or lastingly) put out of action." Even though the separation from home and his arrival in the new surroundings must have seemed sudden to him, he was by no means overwhelmed by them. This "easy to manage" and "undemanding" child (as he was described) for a considerable time kept to his own manner of reacting, his good ego development permitting him to express puzzlement and distress in a sensible fashion, such as conveying his hope to leave by going to the door, by waving "bye-bye." Similarly, the reported "quiet and harmonious relationship" which existed with his mother had equipped his ego to make appropriate bids for attention and to search for substitutes, both functions remaining quite intact even after the experience of separation. On the other hand, it is the constantly repeated frustration of these ego efforts which puts him under strain, and it is the mounting up of the strain which reaches intolerable proportion and finally disrupts his ego. John suffers from a "strain trauma" as defined by Ernst Kris (1956). By the ninth day, all coordinated ego functioning has disappeared; the returning mother finds him almost totally regressed and, without doubt, severely traumatized.

Fascinating as these glimpses are, to me a particular aspect of John's picture supersedes others in importance. What I have in mind is the following:

At the outset of the film story, in Joyce Robertson's words, John is introduced to us as a "bonny and attractive child." There is no doubt that he is well adjusted for his age, his feelings object-directed, his interest in the external world phase-adequate. At the end of the sequence, we see him withdrawn, uncommunicative, out of reach of parental affection, his behavior fluctuating between apathy and listlessness, on the one hand, and wild, aggressive, animallike screaming and struggling, on the other hand. He shows all the characteristics of behavior which are known to us from our contacts with autistic children, a personality change to which we are first alerted in the film when he turns from his search for human objects who are unavailable to the available inanimate ones. To my mind, the most impressive and disturbing scene in the film is the one where he cuddles up to the oversized teddy bear as if it were the mother, not different from the Harlow monkeys who accommodate themselves to the "wire mother" or "cloth mother" offered to them as a substitute.

Autistic children also take the same turn from the animate to the inanimate (or treat the human object as if it were inanimate). Autism, on the other hand, is a disorder of uncertain origin which many of us are reluctant to ascribe to purely psychological, i.e., emotional, causation. The question arises here whether the personality change undergone by John before our eyes should cause us to revise such previously held opinions. Perhaps all autistic children have been potentially normal once, and have been forced back into this ominous state (or kept back in it) by a similar experience of constantly repeated frustration of legitimate needs and expectations. Experiences which at a later and more settled stage may be no more than unhappy, distressing, or depressing may well prove devastating at a time when libidinal and ego functions are on the point of unfolding, i.e., are at their most precarious.

However that may be, we have to feel grateful to the film and the implied urge to keep an open mind, not only on the circumscribed question of autism, but on the whole wide problem of environmental harm.

Whether such early damage to development is irreversible or, if reversible, what traces of it are left behind are questions with which John's parents are much concerned. A follow-up on the child's growth would teach us much in this direction.

15

Painter v. Bannister
Postscript by a Psychoanalyst
(1968)

The case of *Painter v. Bannister*,[1] brought first before a trial court, later before the appellate court, is not different in essence from many cases with which the service in a children's clinic is confronted.

I can imagine plaintiff and defendants, father and grandparents of Mark, in spite of their tug of war, being sufficiently united in their concern for the child to seek expert advice concerning him instead of bringing the matter to

Presented at a seminar on Family Law held jointly with Professor Joseph Goldstein at the Yale Law School, New Haven, April, 1968. It is here published for the first time.

[1] In *Painter v. Bannister* (140 N.W. 2d [Iowa 1966]) a father sought to regain the custody of his seven-year-old son who, at the time of the court decision, had been living with his grandparents for two and a half years following the death of his mother.

the court. If the clinic to which they turned were the Hampstead one (or the Yale Child Study Center), the advice given would be based on psychoanalytic reasoning. The main difference between the legal and the clinical situation then would be that in the first instance the warring partners would have a solution imposed on them, while in the second instance they would be left free either to adopt or to reject the solution with which they are presented.

MARK'S PROBLEM

I do not think that we would find Mark's problem easier to handle than either the trial judge or Mr. Justice Stuart. The issues here are not clear-cut, as they are, for example, in the interest of Laura Neuberger or in the interest of Cindy Brown.[2] Regarding both cases, no child analyst would have a moment's hesitation to decide that these children should not be torn away from "the only effective parent they had ever known." Not so with Mark. Mark was lucky enough to live in normal family circumstances until he was five. There is no reason to suspect that during these decisive years his father did not play the usual important role for him. This "normal" life came to an end only with the disastrous accident which, for reason of their deaths, deprived him of mother and sister and, for other reasons, soon thereafter deprived him of the presence of his father.

Disrupting as the accident was, it does not alter the fact

[2] For the case of Laura Neuberger, see Goldstein and Katz (1965, pp. 1019-1034).

For the case of Cindy Brown, see Goldstein and Katz (1965, pp. 1034-1051) and Writings, Vol. V, ch. 26, iii.

that Mark grew up with parents of his own. We take it for granted that the sudden loss of mother and sibling, coupled with the separation from his father, was deeply upsetting for him. There is no evidence to show how his relations with mother, father, and sister had developed, or how his personality had been shaped before the traumatic moment intervened. That he showed signs of maladjustment after the events, i.e., when he arrived at the grandparents, is not surprising, nor is this necessarily connected with mismanagement on the part of the father or other influences derived from the father's personality. Children frequently react with overt behavior problems to shocks, upsets, and disruptions in their lives, i.e., to events following which adults withdraw into a lengthy mourning process.

MARK'S PAST

In the absence of any other surviving member of the immediate family, the clinic would have to enlist the father's help for clarifying questions concerning Mark's past. We would want to know whether developmental progress was satisfactory or unsatisfactory until age five; whether Mark was in good affectionate contact with his mother, or his father, or with both; whether they considered him a clinging or an independent child; whether before losing his mother, he had reached the stage of obvious preference for her, accompanied by rivalry with and jealousy of his father; whether at this time he had impressed people as a manly or as an unmanly little boy; whether the parents considered him to be a "good" child, age-adequately in control of his impulses, or whether they found him self-indulgent and difficult to manage. Data of this kind would give a clue whether or not the disruption of the family had caused him to undergo a change of personality.

Other relevant information concerning Mark would have to be elicited in the clinic's usual manner from the boy himself. The investigator would have to piece together in particular the residues of his infantile love life. What methods did Mark adopt to cope with his losses? Has he forgotten, denied, or repressed all memories of events before the accident? How far is the image of his dead mother still alive in his mind? Does it or does it not play an important role in his conscious fantasies or, perhaps inaccessible to consciousness, in his unconscious? To what extent has he transferred the feelings for his mother to his grandmother? If he has done so in an intense way, how would he react to a further separation, this time from her? Are there signs to be noted that he would be able to shift his affections, this time to a stepmother who is, so far, unknown to him?

A series of similar questions will arise with regard to Mark's relations with his father. A period of three years, or even one and a half years, is long if measured by the standards of a young child. The experience of being left by a parent, for whatever reason, creates in children a whole host of conflicting emotions, on the one hand sorrow and longing, on the other hand despair, anger, and resentment. In some cases the negative feelings gain the upper hand and extinguish the affection. In others the opposite happens: love for the absent parent is increased beyond all measure, and the child remains tied to him.

As regards Mark, we have no evidence so far to show what happened in his case. There is the contention that the boy's allegiance to his father has been transferred in its entirety to the grandfather. If this were proved to be true, inquiry would still be needed whether this shift was a wholly positive one or whether it was prompted, at least in part, by the boy's anger with the absent father, an anger which may well be smoldering under the surface and may burst out some time to the detriment of his development.

THE WARRING ADULTS

Since in the clinical situation both parties in the dispute have consulted us of their own free will, we can also count on their cooperation in investigating their own respective attitudes toward the child. Clinical and analytic experience teaches us that children can fill many different roles in the emotional lives of their parents or of other adults. They may be no more for them than a piece of property which is valued egoistically as an extension of the adult's personality; when this happens they serve the adult's needs, while their own developmental needs remain unconsidered. In contrast to this, they may be loved unselfishly, as persons in their own right, with their own needs of paramount importance. Further, they may be no more than a pawn in a game, with no importance of their own, except that possession or dispossession of their persons signifies victory or defeat for the warring factions. The boy Larry in *Lesser v. Lesser* is a case in kind.[3]

With Mark's father and grandparents it is difficult to foresee the result of our investigations. In the father, there are signs of obvious, object-directed feelings for the child, alternating with periods of detachment, which may or may

[3] See Goldstein and Katz (1965, Chapter 1) and *Writings*, Vol. V, ch. 26.

not be attributable to the man's immediate reaction to his tragic losses. On the other hand, there are also indications that, as a father, he is not disinclined to use his son selfishly, i.e., for his own aggrandizement as an author, a figure on TV, etc.

As for the grandparents, we are prepared to find that for them Mark represents the daughter whom they have lost and mourn. There is also the suspicion that in claiming Mark, they reclaim symbolically their daughter from the son-in-law, who from the start was unwelcome to them for many reasons. There also is little doubt that the grandparents love Mark himself, are attentive to his needs, and sacrifice for him some of the peace and quiet of their home-life to which every elderly couple is entitled.

The weight and truth of any of these pronouncements remain tentative until they are confirmed or disputed by probing interviews with the three adults in question.

LEGAL V. PSYCHOANALYTIC ASPECTS

Unlike the two courts, we are in the lucky position not to have to pronounce judgment. We merely formulate advice. When doing so, we disregard or minimize the importance of some of the facts which swayed the courts.

In disagreement with the trial judge, and in agreement with his expert, Dr. Hawks, we discount the importance of the "biological father" as such. The "blood ties" between parent and child as well as the alleged paternal and maternal "instincts" are biological concepts which, only too often, prove vague and unreliable when transferred to the field of psychology. Psychologically speaking, the child's "father" is the adult man to whom the child attaches a particular, psychologically distinctive set of feelings. When this type of emotional tie is disrupted, the child's feelings suffer. When such separations occur during phases of development in which the child is particularly vulnerable, the whole foundation of his personality may be shaken. The presence of or the reunion with a biological father to whom no such ties exist will not recompense the child for the loss which he has suffered. Conversely, the biological father's or mother's unselfish love for their child is by no means to be taken for granted. It happens often enough that biological parents fail in their duty to the child, while other adults who are less closely related to him, i.e., who have no "instinctive" basis for their feelings, successfully take over the parental role.

We place less emphasis than Mr. Justice Stuart on benefits such as a "stable, dependable background" with educational and professional opportunities. Important as such external advantages are, we have seen too often that they can be wasted unless they are accompanied by the internal emotional constellations which enable the children to profit from them. Children are known to thrive in socially and financially unstable situations if they are firmly attached to their parents, and to come to grief under the best social conditions when such emotional security is missing.

We are in agreement with Mr. Justice Stuart concerning the inadvisability of gambling with a child's future. So long as development seems to proceed well, we—like he—feel reluctant to interfere. On the other hand, on the basis of clinical experience, we have learned that in this respect, as in many others, surface appearances may be misleading.

FORMULATION OF ADVICE

It is not possible at this point to foretell whether, after investigation, our advice will be in line with the judgment of the trial court or with Mr. Justice Stuart. What can be promised is that it will be based not on external facts but on internal data. We shall advise that Mark had better stay with his grandparents provided that the following facts can be ascertained:

> that the transfer of his attachment from the parents to the grandparents is fairly complete and promises to be permanent during his childhood; i.e., that they have become the central figures toward whom his feelings are directed and around whom his emotional life revolves (in psychoanalytic terms: his objects, cathected in the normal way with libido and aggression, his models for identification, etc.);
>
> that, given this new attachment, a further change is not advisable; instead of being profitable, it would disturb the present equilibrium by opening up old memories, by re-creating a situation of upset, bewilderment, and need for new adaptation, this time to a stepmother who is, so far, unknown;
>
> that the grandparents, on their part, cherish Mark for his own sake, not only as a replacement for the daughter who was killed, nor as a pawn in the battle with their son-in-law.

Conversely, we shall advise that Mark had better be returned to his father if the following facts emerge:

> that Mr. Painter still retains his place as "father" in Mark's mind and that in spite of separation and new

experiences the child's feelings and fantasies continue
to revolve around him;

that anger about the "desertion" (and perhaps blame for
the mother's death) have not succeeded in turning this
relationship into a predominantly hostile one;

that the father cherishes Mark for his own sake;

that it can be shown that Mr. Painter's using the child
for publicity purposes was not due to lack of paternal
consideration on his part but happened owing to the
bitterness and resentment caused by the fight for possession of his son.

Provided that Mr. Painter, Mr. and Mrs. Bannister, and
Mark would allow the clinic two or three weeks' time for
investigation, I am confident that we should be able to
guide them toward a potentially helpful solution of their
difficult problem.

16

Address at the Commencement Services of the Yale Law School (1968)

I share with you, the students who graduate from the Yale Law School today, a feeling of deep gratitude for the University which has given us a great deal: to you the opportunity to learn and equip yourselves for a future career; to me the opportunity to enter into a new field of work, to teach, and, incidentally, to acquire a further degree, in a world in which degree and consequent status count for much. Relying on this common experience, I use this last opportunity before your departure to look back on our time together, hoping that you will carry some residue of it with you into your professional lives.

On this occasion the author was awarded an honorary degree. The address is published here for the first time.

As you well know, our two disciplines, the law and psychoanalysis, have approached each other very cautiously and diffidently, with the links between them few and far between. To begin with, they were wholly divided and seemed destined to remain that way for good reasons. Legal concepts are time-honored, clear-cut, concise, well defined, and based on indisputable facts; contrasted with them, psychoanalytic tenets are vague, diffuse, complex, and rooted in the revolutionary assumption of a dynamic unconscious mind. No wonder that there was—and still is—the widespread conviction that to include in legal teaching some thinking about the psychology of the human beings to whom the laws are applied is at best unprofitable and at worst leads to confusion.

It is in the face of such opposition that psychology nevertheless is finding two openings for entry into the fabric of the law: into criminal law via the *insanity defense*, a concept which cannot be defined except in psychiatric terms; and into family law via the much used slogan of *the best interests of the child*, which conceptually belongs in the realm of developmental psychology. At least, so far as these two branches of the law are concerned, ideas about the working of the human mind, even if in rudimentary form, have come to stay.

Among the very small number of law schools to admit this fact, yours was foremost. Luckily for me, your teachers guided you through this inevitable first phase of almost grudging acknowledgment of human complexities before I ever came to visit.

There were plenty of obstacles to mutual understanding that remained for us even after the initial breakthrough had been made. Nothing can alter the fact that psychoanalytic investigations are oriented essentially toward the deeper, unconscious layers of the mind and are aimed at unraveling *motivation*, whereas legal thinking disregards any hidden reasons for behavior and concerns itself with *acts* as well as with the harmful consequences of those acts to the social setting within which they occur. So long as one discipline (i.e., psychoanalysis) considers as negligible the very facts which are of overriding importance to the other (i.e., the law), any cooperation between representatives of the two fields is bound to lead to the heated discussions in which we were involved frequently.

There was also a further reason why we often found each other at cross-purposes. Since your professional education took place within the framework of the adversary system, you tended to misconstrue the intentions of the psychoanalyst who has been taught to think dispassionately and without ulterior motives. You assumed automatically that, when he tries to understand and explain the working of the criminal mind, he takes the stand as counsel for the defense, and that to make allowances for his views is equivalent with successful pleas for the wrongdoers and inevitably leads to a world of "crime without punishment." To uphold law and order you felt obliged to argue for the prosecution and this, quite unnecessarily, brought with it the acrimony which commonly governs legal battles.

I hope that, in the course of my three visits to Yale, we have succeeded in also taking a next step which leads us out of the various controversies onto some safer, common ground. What we share, after all, as psychoanalysts on one side and as future lawyers and judges on the other, is the fact that all of us deal with human failures. In our psychoanalytic practice we handle people who have not come to

terms with themselves and who, consequently, inflict symptomatology and mental suffering on their own persons.
You, in your future legal practice, will in many instances
deal with people who have not come to terms with the
demands of the community within which they live and
who, consequently, constitute a threat to their environment. There are also those individuals who fall between
the two categories, come into our hands when they behave
as "ill" people, and fall under your jurisdiction when they
behave "dissocially," their same internal difficulties manifesting themselves sometimes in the one, at other times in
the other direction. While we try to protect our patients
from the harm which they are doing to themselves, it is
your task to safeguard society by keeping criminal activity
in check. That for these different purposes different means
have to be employed, goes without saying.

There are also some further questions which transcend
the practical and assume importance within the realm of
unsolved theoretical problems. We do not know so far
which sequence of events in human life we should consider
normal. It is an attractive thought that it might be necessary for each of us, as individuals, to solve our internal
conflicts and establish an inner peace and equilibrium before we can comply wholeheartedly with the exigencies of
the environment and become truly social beings. Nevertheless, the facts, as we uncover them in the study of the very
young, point in the opposite direction. It seems rather that
all of us start out in life in an initial state of utter lawless-
ness; that the battles with those nearest to us, i.e., our
parents, educate us gradually toward compliance; and that
this compliance with the external world becomes the precondition for internal conflict. Seen in this light, our psy-

choanalytic patients (the neurotics) live on a higher developmental plane of inner strife, while your clients, the lawbreakers, either have never arrived at this or, at some time or other, have regressed from it to the more primitive form of battle with the world around them.

I think you will concur with me that, on this level of thinking, the disagreements between us disappear and make way for a common effort to increase understanding of the phenomena which are before us.

Part III

17

Foreword to *The Hampstead
Clinic Psychoanalytic Library
Series*
(1969 [1968])

The series of publications of which the present volume
forms a part will be welcomed by all those readers who are
concerned with the history of psychoanalytic concepts and
interested in following the vicissitudes of their fate through
the theoretical, clinical, and technical writings of psychoanalytic authors. On the one hand, these fates may strike
us as being very different from each other. On the other
hand, it proves not too difficult to single out some common
trends and to explore the reasons for them.

First published in *Basic Psychoanalytic Concepts on the Libido
Theory* [The Hampstead Clinic Psychoanalytic Library, Volume
I], edited by Humberto Nagera et al. London: George Allen &
Unwin; New York: Basic Books, 1969.

There are some terms and concepts which served an important function for psychoanalysis in its earliest years because of their being simple and all-embracing, for example, the notion of a *complex*. Even the lay public understood more or less easily that what was meant thereby was any cluster of impulses, emotions, thoughts, etc., which have their roots in the unconscious and, exerting their influence from there, give rise to anxiety, defenses, and symptom formation in the conscious mind. Accordingly, the term was used widely as a form of psychological shorthand. "Father complex," "mother complex," "guilt complex," "inferiority complex," etc., became familiar notions. Nevertheless, in due course, added psychoanalytic findings about the child's relationship to his parents, about the early mother-infant tie and its consequences, about the complexities of lacking self-esteem and feelings of insufficiency and inferiority demanded more precise conceptualization. The very omnibus nature of the term could not but lead to its, at least partial, abandonment. All that remained from it were the terms "oedipus complex" to designate the experiences centered around the triangular relationships of the phallic phase, and "castration complex" for the anxieties, repressed wishes, etc., concerning the loss or lack of the male sexual organ.

If, in the former instance, a general concept was split up to make room for more specific meanings, in other instances concepts took turns in the opposite direction. After starting out as concrete, well-defined descriptions of circumscribed psychic events, they were applied by many authors to an ever-widening circle of phenomena until their connotation became increasingly vague and imprecise and until finally special efforts had to be made to redefine them, to restrict their sphere of application, and to invest them once more with precision and significance. This is what happened, for example, to the concepts of *transference* and of *trauma*.

The concept and the term "transference" were originally designed to establish the fact that the realistic relationship between analyst and patient is invariably distorted by fantasies and object relations which stem from the patient's past, and that these very distortions can be turned into a technical tool to reveal the patient's past pathogenic history. At present, the meaning of the term has been widened to the extent that it comprises whatever happens between analyst and patient regardless of its derivation and of the reasons for its happening.

A "trauma" or "traumatic happening" originally meant an (external or internal) event of a magnitude with which the individual's ego is unable to deal, i.e., a sudden influx of excitation, massive enough to break through the ego's normal stimulus barrier. To this purely quantitative meaning of the term were added in time all sorts of qualifications (such as cumulative, retrospective, silent, beneficial), until the concept ended up as more or less synonymous with the notion of a pathogenic event in general (see *Writings*, Vol. V, ch. 14).

Psychoanalytic concepts may also be overtaken by a further fate, which is perhaps of even greater significance. Most of them owe their origin to a particular era of psychoanalytic theory, or to a particular field of clinical application, or to a particular mode of technique. Since any of the backgrounds in which they are rooted, are open to change, this should lead either to a corresponding change in the concepts or to their abandonment. But, most frequently, this has failed to happen. Many concepts are carried forward through the changing scene of psychoanalytic theory and practice without sufficient thought being given to their necessary alteration or redefinition. This has been the case with regard to the concept of acting out (see ch. 7 in this volume).

It was in this state of affairs that Humberto Nagera initiated his inquiry into the history of psychoanalytic thinking. Assisted by a team of analytic workers, trained in the Hampstead Child-Therapy Course and Clinic, he set out to trace the course of basic psychoanalytic concepts from their first appearance through their changes in the 23 Volumes of the *Standard Edition of the Complete Psychological Works of Sigmund Freud*, i.e., to a point from where they are meant to be taken further to include the writings of the most important authors of the post-Freudian era.

Nagera's aim in this venture was a fourfold one:

(i) to facilitate for readers of the psychoanalytic literature the understanding of psychoanalytic thought and of the terminology in which it is expressed;

(ii) to understand and define concepts, not only according to their individual significance, but also according to their relevance to the particular historical phase of psychoanalytic theory within which they have arisen;

(iii) to induce psychoanalytic authors to use their terms and concepts more precisely with regard for the theoretical framework to which they owe their origin, and thereby to reduce the many sources of misunderstanding and confusion which govern the psychoanalytic literature at present;

(iv) finally, to create for students of psychoanalysis the opportunity to embark on a course of independent reading and study, linked to a scholarly aim and designed to promote their critical and constructive thinking on matters of theory formation.

18

Foreword to
"A Psychoanalytic
Contribution to Pediatrics,"
by Bianca Gordon
(1970)

Work with pediatricians and hospital personnel does not belong to the early extensions of psychoanalytic activity. The application of psychoanalytic child psychology moved very gradually from the understanding of the child's emotional relationships within the family to the understanding of his behavior in nursery school and school, his learning potentialities and inhibitions, his first ties with playmates, his first encounter with community standards, his compliance with or revolt against the teachers' authority. In

First published in *The Psychoanalytic Study of the Child*, 25: 521-523, 1970.

accordance with the specialization of work in the children's field which obtained at the time, this knowledge was shared only with the professional workers who were engaged with the psychological side of the child's life such as nursery school teachers, teachers, child guidance and juvenile court personnel, while concern with the child's or adolescent's physical health or ill-health remained strictly a medical concern, untouched by insight into the complicating emotional factors.

The gap between mental and physical aspects of child development was closed then, increasingly, due to two separate advances in the psychoanalytic study of the child. One was the move of investigation from the later to the earlier years of childhood, especially to the first and second year. At this period of life any mental experience such as anxiety, distress, impatience, rage, frustration, etc., may be discharged in the form of physical upsets such as the disturbance of sleep, food intake, elimination, etc., while any bodily discomfort, pains, intestinal upsets may cause emotional upheavals in the form of unhappiness, distress, anxiety. In short, psychosomatic reactions are the order of the day, and the links between physical and mental processes are inescapable for the analytic observer.

The second line of inquiry was concerned with older children and the fluctuations in growth and structuralization of the personality which are due to the general influence of bodily illness on mental development. What was explored in detail was the meaning to the child of a massive influx of unpleasure, of motor and dietary restrictions, of surgical interventions, of nursing care, etc., with special regard for the regressions in libidinal phase development and ego functioning, which are the frequent consequences of experiences of this nature.

Nevertheless, it remained difficult to engage the medical world's interest in these studies, and the first effective breakthrough in this respect was made, not on the basis of such interactions between body and mind, but via the plight of ill children who have to be taken to a hospital. It was the emphatic description of the *separation anxiety* of hospitalized infants which succeeded finally to convince a number of doctors and nurses that, to be therapeutically effective, the care for a child's ill body needs to be complemented by concern for and attention to his psychological needs. In fact, the general public's readiness to acknowledge the importance of separation anxiety threatened for a while to overshadow the equally important impact of the illnesses themselves.

To set the record straight again, it needed systematic work as described by Bianca Gordon (1970) and carried out by her in connection with the outpatient and inpatient departments of major children's hospitals. Perhaps, in the distant future new training programs in pediatrics and nursing will equip all hospital staff with sufficient knowledge of emotional factors to insure enlightened management of their child patients. But, until the time when this happens, pediatricians will have to rely on consultation with a psychoanalytically trained advisor; ward sisters and nurses will need instruction and guidance of the same kind; medical social workers and hospital teachers will learn from such help to use their professional skills to the best advantage. Above all, as illustrated by Gordon's paper, the psychoanalytic consultant will be an indispensable figure in the maternity wards and infant clinics where the opportunities for preventive work are almost limitless.

Such work is already being carried out in some selected centers in England as well as in the United States. But it is still waiting for its introduction into children's hospitals, pediatric wards, and infant welfare clinics on the widest scale.

19

Foreword to *The Wolf-Man* by the Wolf-Man
(1971)

As readers of the literature of psychoanalysis, we are impressed by the large number of papers, books, and periodicals in various languages which cover a wide range of topics: clinical, technical, theoretical, as well as the applications of analytic insight to the fields of psychiatry, general medicine, pediatrics, education, culture, religion, literature, the arts, the law, etc. Nevertheless, we cannot help being conscious at the same time of a conspicuous contrasting dearth of publications in a specific direction: that of complete and adequately documented case histories.

This failure in output where the practicing analyst's main preoccupation is concerned is not attributable to the fact that analysts know too little of their patients but to the

First published in *The Wolf-Man* by the Wolf-Man, ed. Muriel Gardiner. New York: Basic Books, 1971, pp. ix-xii.

opposite—that they know too much. The technical tools of analytic therapy such as free association, dream interpretation, resistance and transference interpretations produce a mass of data about the patient's life history, the healthy and the pathological sides of his nature, which, due to its bulk, is unwieldy and, if written up in undigested form, unreadable. To handle this raw material in a manner which produces, on the one hand, the vivid image of an individual person and, on the other hand, a detailed picture of a specific psychological disorder is no mean task and, as a literary achievement, far beyond the powers of most scientific authors. What is produced accordingly in our day are either snippets of clinical material used to illustrate some theoretical conception or, at best, one-sided clinical accounts which fail to acquaint the reader with the patient as a living personality. It is not surprising therefore that, for teaching purposes, the lecturers and seminar leaders of our institutes developed the habit of falling back on the small number of classical case histories which we possess and exploited them to the utmost. Anna O. and the others from the *Studies on Hysteria*, Little Hans, the Rat Man, the Wolf Man, Schreber, Dora, thus became well known to every succeeding generation of analysts, together with the lessons learned from them concerning conversion hysteria, phobia, obsessional states, the infantile neuroses, paranoia, homosexuality, etc.

On the other hand, the success in summarizing, condensing, selecting, and synthesizing material, which made these stories so eminently readable, also had some unsuspected results. The very familiarity which analysts began to feel with these patients aroused the temptation to deal with them in their imagination as if they were their own patients, to wish to know everything about them, to test the interpretations given, to probe beyond the conclusions drawn, and wherever possible to reconstitute once more the original data from which the author's abstractions had been made. The central figures of the classical case histories thus became focal points for speculation and discussion among analysts, with the desire uppermost to extend every one of these treatments into a longitudinal study by undertaking follow-ups, a difficult task since it presupposed establishing identities which had been disguised more or less effectively for reasons of discretion.

We have learned through Ellen Jensen's papers on Anna O. about her later life, work, and fame, and have to conclude from this that her "talking cure" was efficient enough to remove the crippling symptomatology of her severe affliction, despite the fact that the transference to her physician had remained uninterpreted. We would like to be informed whether the "wild analysis" undertaken with Katharina had the effect of counteracting the consequences of her traumatic seduction and observation and enabled her to embark on a normal life, but in her case no one succeeded in penetrating the mystery of her identity. As regards Frau Emmy von N., some information about her later life and personal reactions was unearthed. Little Hans, whose identity had never been obscure to the same degree, is now known to have reached a secure and reputable social position, that is, outwardly unhindered by any phobic limitations, although there is no telling from the manifest picture whether or not the infantile neurosis left any deeper aftereffects on his personality. Where the original data for the analysis were available *in toto*, as in the Schreber case, this led to later extensions, reinterpretations, critical reviews, etc. Nevertheless, although in these investigations no efforts were spared, the actual results remained meager, abortive, and, for this reason, unsatisfactory to any analyst's questing mind.

This, then, is the gap in knowledge which the present publication serves to fill in an admirable way. The Wolf Man stands out among his fellow figures by virtue of the fact that he is the only one able and willing to cooperate actively in the reconstruction and follow-up of his own case. He is not shrouded in mystery like Katharina, nor estranged and inimical toward his former therapy like Anna O., nor reticent and shy of publicity like the adult Little Hans. His grateful respect for and ready understanding of analytic thinking lifted him, according to his own testimony, already during his initial treatment from the status of a patient to that of a younger colleague of his analyst, a collaborator with "an experienced explorer setting out to study a new, recently discovered land." Moreover, he succeeded in maintaining this spirit which had carried him through the resistances of his first analysis; and after losing it temporarily during his subsequent character changes and treatment, managed to regain it so that he was able to endure the turbulence of a life interfered with by revolutions, wars, material deprivations, and traumatic object losses. What he proudly reports as his analyst's acknowledgment of his first-class intelligence not only stood him in good stead throughout his personal life but also was instrumental in benefiting the psychoanalytic community as a whole in an unprecedented manner.

We owe Ruth Mack Brunswick a debt of gratitude for adding the account of his postanalytic disturbance to the original story of his infantile neurosis. We owe an equally great or even greater debt now to Muriel Gardiner, who took up the task where it had been left by her two predecessors, who befriended the Wolf Man for more than thirty years, supported him in his depressions, dealt patiently with his misgivings, doubts, and uncertainties, encouraged him in his self-expressions and autobiographical revelations, and finally compiled and edited the disconnected sequences which were produced.

The result of her labors is what we have before us: the unique opportunity to see an analytic patient's inner as well as outer life unfold before our eyes, starting out from his own childhood memories and the picture of his childhood neurosis, taking us through the major and minor incidents of his adulthood, and leading from there, almost uninterruptedly, to a concluding period when "The Wolf-Man Grows Older."

20

James Strachey
(1969)

It cannot be easy for any man to give up his own personal
pursuits for the purpose of immersing himself wholly in the
work of another. But this is, in fact, what James Strachey
undertook and achieved to do. In his middle years he had
already acquired considerable status as a clinical analyst, as
a teacher in the British Institute for Psycho-Analysis, as a
leading figure in the British Psycho-Analytical Society and
the International Psycho-Analytical Association, as the author of scientific papers. All these activities were abandoned by him when he decided to become the translator of
Freud's Complete Works, and when he followed up this
decision by withdrawing into voluntary seclusion, i.e., into
the form of life which seemed to him best suited to the
task.

First published in the *International Journal of Psycho-Analysis*,
50:129-131, 1969.

To translate any scientific matter is fraught with difficulties of all kinds. What is needed, obviously, is a thorough knowledge of both languages in question as well as familiarity with the subject matter. There is the widespread conviction that most translators miss out on one or the other of these requirements, if not on all three. But even where the translator is thoroughly equipped, the work is hard at best, and frustrating and unrewarding at its worst.

Expression in one language does not lend itself automatically to expression in another. What is natural to a German author such as allusions, similes, imagery, etc., sounds flowery and unsuitable to the English reader; conversely, what counts as precise in English, strikes the German reader as barren and arid. There are always idioms which defy translation. Quotations which are familiar to the readers in one culture lack appeal when carried over into another. There are also the local nuances of expression which baffle any foreigner who has been taught the language according to another local usage, the differences between South and North Germany being a case in point. Accordingly, every translator finds himself faced with the dilemma whether to render a "free" version of his text, which may be condemned as arbitrary, or a faithful, verbally irreproachable one which plays havoc with the original author's flow of style.

James Strachey was able to overcome these obstacles and to pursue his way due to a rare combination of linguistic capability, stylistic mastery, scholarly exactness, and psychoanalytic erudition. His ambition went far beyond that of the mere translator. What he set out to do was to conjure up for the English-speaking public the whole conceptual world of psychoanalysis, to widen the existing language where it was unable to accommodate the new notions, and, simultaneously, to hold the right middle line between coining a precise and indispensable technical terminology and expressing complex thoughts in simple words.

That he regarded the task essentially as a creative one is borne out by the fact that he firmly refused to pass as correct and to include any of the earlier English translations, whether produced by others or himself. According to his plan, the final product had to be uniform, homogeneous, all of one piece, i.e., the considered product of a single mind.

It is difficult to judge now, at a later date, whether in Strachey's own mind his role as translator had precedence over that of editor and commentator, or whether his interest had taken the opposite course. However that may be, in the final product of the Standard Edition the two activities go hand in hand. It is the reader's impression that the translator's preoccupation with the original text and its rendering led him to see logical sequences and historical connections which otherwise would have gone unnoticed and which, in many instances, were probably unknown to Freud himself. This is invaluable for the student of psychoanalysis who is concerned with tracing the gradual development of the new discipline, the shifts and changes of thought which made up its growth, the links between clinical experience and theoretical formulations, etc.

The founder of psychoanalysis is considered fortunate to have found a translator of this stature. It may also be said that James Strachey was fortunate to find an author and a subject matter worthy of his efforts.

Bibliography

AICHHORN, A. (1925), *Wayward Youth*. New York: Viking Press, 1935.

ALEXANDER, F. & STAUB, H. (1929), *The Criminal, the Judge, and the Public*. New York: Macmillan, 1931.

BALINT, M. (1958), The Three Areas of the Mind. *Int. J. Psycho-Anal.*, 39:328-340.

BENEDEK, T., see FLEMING, J.

BERNFELD, S. (1924), *Vom dichterischen Schaffen der Jugend*. Vienna: Internationaler psychoanalytischer Verlag.

—— (1930), *Der analytische Unterricht für Pädagogen*. Vienna: Internationaler psychoanalytischer Verlag.

BIBRING, E. (1936), The Development and Problems of the Theory of the Instincts. *Int. J. Psycho-Anal.*, 22:102-131, 1941.

—— (1937), On the Theory of the Therapeutic Results of Psycho-Analysis. *Int. J. Psycho-Anal.*, 18:170-189.

BIBRING, G. L. (1966), Old Age: Its Liabilities and Its Assets. In: *Psychoanalysis—A General Psychology*, ed. R. M. Loewenstein, L. M. Newman, M. Schur, & A. J. Solnit. New York: International Universities Press, pp. 253-271.

BORNSTEIN, B. (1930a), Beziehungen zwischen Sexual- und Intellektentwicklung. *Z. psychoanal. Päd.*, 4:446-454.

—— (1930b), Zur Psychogenese der Pseudodebilität. *Int. Z. Psychoanal.*, 16:378-399.

BORNSTEIN, S. (1933), A Child Analysis. *Psychoanal. Quart.*, 4:190-225.

BRENNER, C. (1968), Archaic Features of Ego Functioning. *Int. J. Psycho-Anal.*, 49:426-429.

BREUER, J. & FREUD, S. (1893-1895), Studies on Hysteria. *Standard Edition*, 2.*

BURLINGHAM, D. (1951), *Twins: A Study of Three Pairs of Identical Twins*. New York: International Universities Press.

—— & FREUD, A. (1942), *Young Children in War-Time*. London: George Allen & Unwin.

—— —— (1944), *Infants Without Families*. London: George Allen & Unwin.

CALDWELL, B. (1966), A Day Care Program for Fostering Cognitive Development. In: *On Rearing Infants and Young Children in Institutions*, ed. H. L. Witmer. Washington: U.S. Dept. of H.E.W., Children's Bureau Research Reports, No. 1, 1967, pp. 33-40.

COBLINER, W. G., *see* SPITZ, R. A.

DEMENT, W. (1960), Effect of Dream Deprivation. *Science*, 131:1705-1707.

—— & FISHER, C. (1963), Experimental Interference with the Sleep Cycle. *Canad. Psychiat. Assn. J.*, 8:400-405.

—— *see also* FISHER, C.

DERSHOWITZ, A. M., *see* KATZ, J.

DONNELLY, R. C., GOLDSTEIN, J., & SCHWARTZ, R. D. (1962), *Criminal Law*. New York: Free Press.

EISSLER, K. R. (1953), The Effect of the Structure of the Ego on Psychoanalytic Technique. *J. Amer. Psychoanal. Assn.*, 1:104-143.

ERIKSON, E. H. (1950), *Childhood and Society*. New York; Norton, rev. ed., 1963.

ESCALONA, S. K. (1966), Developmental Needs of Children under Two-and-a-Half Years Old. In: *On Rearing Infants and*

*See footnote‡.

Young Children in Institutions, ed. H. L. Witmer. Washington: U.S. Dept. of H.E.W., Children's Bureau Research Reports, No. 1, 1967, pp. 7-13.

FEDERN, P. (1952), *Ego Psychology and the Psychoses.* New York: Basic Books.

FENICHEL, O. (1937), Symposium on the Theory of the Therapeutic Results of Psychoanalysis. *The Collected Papers of Otto Fenichel,* 2:19-24. New York: Norton, 1954.

FERENCZI, S. (1920), Open Letter. *Int. J. Psycho-Anal.,* 1:1-2.

FISHER, C. (1965), Psychoanalytic Implications of Recent Research on Sleep and Dreaming. *J. Amer. Psychoanal. Assn.,* 13:197-303.

——— & DEMENT, W. (1963), Studies on the Psychopathology of Sleep and Dreams. *Amer. J. Psychiat.,* 119:1160-1168.

——— *see also* DEMENT, W.

FLEMING, J. & BENEDEK, T. (1966), *Psychoanalytic Supervision.* New York: Grune & Stratton.

FREUD, ANNA (1926-1927), *Introduction to the Technique of Child Analysis.* New York: Nervous and Mental Disease Monograph No. 48, 1929; also in: *The Psycho-Analytical Treatment of Children.* New York: International Universities Press, 1959 [see Volume I†].

——— (1930), *Psychoanalysis for Teachers and Parents.* New York: Emerson Books [see Volume I].

——— (1936), *The Ego and the Mechanisms of Defense.* New York: International Universities Press, rev. ed. 1966 [Volume II].

——— (1965), *Normality and Pathology in Childhood: Assessments of Development.* New York: International Universities Press [Volume VI].

——— (1968), *Indications for Child Analysis and Other Papers.* New York: International Universities Press [Volume IV].

——— (1969), *Research at the Hampstead Child-Therapy Clinic and Other Papers.* New York: International Universities Press [Volume V].

† The Volume numbers in brackets refer to *The Writings of Anna Freud.* New York: International Universities Press, 1966-

—— see also BURLINGHAM, D.

FREUD, SIGMUND (1895), Project for a Scientific Psychology. *The Origins of Psychoanalysis*. New York: Basic Books, 1954.

—— (1905a [1901]), Fragment of an Analysis of a Case of Hysteria. *Standard Edition*, 7:3-122.‡

—— (1905b), Three Essays on the Theory of Sexuality. *Standard Edition*, 7:125-243.

—— (1909), Analysis of a Phobia in a Five-Year-Old Boy. *Standard Edition*, 10:3-149.

—— (1911-1915), Papers on Technique. *Standard Edition*, 12:85-173.

—— (1914), Remembering, Repeating and Working-Through. *Standard Edition*, 12:145-156.

—— (1917), A Difficulty in the Path of Psycho-Analysis. *Standard Edition*, 17: 135-144.

—— (1918 [1914]), From the History of an Infantile Neurosis. *Standard Edition*, 17:3-123.

—— (1923), The Ego and the Id. *Standard Edition*, 19:3-66.

—— (1924), The Economic Problem of Masochism. *Standard Edition*, 19:157-170.

—— (1925 [1924]), The Resistances to Psycho-Analysis. *Standard Edition*, 19:213-222.

—— (1926a [1925]), Inhibitions, Symptoms and Anxiety. *Standard Edition*, 20:77-174.

—— (1926b), The Question of Lay Analysis. *Standard Edition*, 20:179-258.

—— (1930 [1929]), Civilization and Its Discontents. *Standard Edition*, 21:59-145.

—— (1933 [1932]), New Introductory Lectures on Psycho-Analysis. *Standard Edition*, 22:3-182.

—— (1937), Analysis Terminable and Interminable. *Standard Edition*, 23:209-253.

—— see also BREUER, J.

‡ *The Standard Edition of the Complete Psychological Works of Sigmund Freud*, 24 Volumes, translated and edited by James Strachey. London: Hogarth Press and the Institute of Psycho-Analysis, 1953-

FREUD, W. E. (1967), Assessment of Early Infancy: Problems and Considerations. *The Psychoanalytic Study of the Child*, 22:216-238.§

FURST, S. S., ed. (1967), *Psychic Trauma*. New York: Basic Books.

GAVRIN, J. (1966), An Institution for Young Children. In: *On Rearing Infants and Young Children in Institutions*, ed. H. L. Witmer. Washington: U.S. Dept. of H.E.W., Children's Bureau Research Reports, No. 1, 1967, pp. 28-33.

GILL, M. M., see RAPAPORT, D.

GOLDSTEIN, A. S. (1967), *The Insanity Defense*. New Haven: Yale University Press.

GOLDSTEIN, J. & KATZ, J. (1965), *The Family and the Law: Problems for Decision in the Family Law Process*. New York: Free Press.

———— see also DONNELLY, R. C., and KATZ, J.

GORDON, B. (1970), A Psychoanalytic Contribution to Pediatrics. *The Psychoanalytic Study of the Child*, 25:521-543.

GREENACRE, P. (1967), The Influence of Infantile Trauma on Genetic Patterns. In: *Psychic Trauma*, ed. S. S. Furst. New York: Basic Books, pp. 108-153.

GREENSON, R. R. (1958), Variations in Classical Psycho-Analytic Technique: An Introduction. *Int. J. Psycho-Anal.*, 39:200-201.

———— (1967), *The Technique and Practice of Psychoanalysis*. New York: International Universities Press.

HARLOW, H. F. (1959), Love in Infant Monkeys. *Sci. Amer.*, 200(6):68-74.

———— & ZIMMERMAN, R. R. (1959), Affectional Responses in the Infant Monkey. *Science*, 130:421-432.

HARTMANN, E. (1967), *The Biology of Dreaming*. Springfield: Charles C Thomas.

§ *The Psychoanalytic Study of the Child*, currently 25 Volumes, edited by Ruth S. Eissler, Anna Freud, Heinz Hartmann, Marianne Kris, Seymour L. Lustman. New York: International Universities Press; London: Hogarth Press, 1945-1970.

HARTMANN, H. (1939), *Ego Psychology and the Problem of Adaptation.* New York: International Universities Press, 1958.

——— (1964), *Essays on Ego Psychology.* New York: International Universities Press.

HEIMANN, P. (1950), On Counter-Transference. *Int. J. Psycho-Anal.,* 31:81-84.

HOEDEMAKER, F., *see* KALES, A.

HOFFER, W. (1952), The Mutual Influences in the Development of Ego and Id: Earliest Stages. *The Psychoanalytic Study of the Child,* 7:31-41.

JACOBSON, A., *see* KALES, A.

JACOBSON, E. (1964), *The Self and the Object World.* New York: International Universities Press.

JAMES, M. (1960), Premature Ego Development: Some Observations upon Disturbances in the First Three Years of Life. *Int. J. Psycho-Anal.,* 41:288-294.

JOHNSON, V. E., *see* MASTERS, W. H.

JONES, E. (1957), *The Life and Work of Sigmund Freud,* Vol. 3. New York: Basic Books.

KALES, A., HOEDEMAKER, F., JACOBSON, A., & LICHTENSTEIN, E. (1964), Dream-deprivation: An Experimental Reappraisal. *Nature* (London), 204:1337-1338.

KATZ, J., GOLDSTEIN, J., & DERSHOWITZ, A. M. (1967), *Psychoanalysis, Psychiatry and Law.* New York: Free Press.

——— *see also* GOLDSTEIN, J.

KHAN, M. M. R. (1963), The Concept of Cumulative Trauma. *The Psychoanalytic Study of the Child,* 18:286-306.

KINSEY, A. C. ET AL. (1948), *Sexual Behavior in the Human Male.* Philadelphia: Saunders.

KLEIN, M. (1921-1945), *Contributions to Psycho-Analysis.* London: Hogarth Press.

KOHUT, H. (1970), Scientific Activities of the American Psychoanalytic Association: An Inquiry. *J. Amer. Psychoanal. Assn.,* 18:462-484.

KRIS, E. (1950), Notes on the Development and on Some Current Problems of Psychoanalytic Child Psychology. *The Psychoanalytic Study of the Child,* 5:24-46.

—— (1951), Opening Remarks on Psychoanalytic Child Psychology. *The Psychoanalytic Study of the Child*, 6:9-17.

—— (1955), Neutralization and Sublimation: Observations on Young Children. *The Psychoanalytic Study of the Child*, 10:30-46.

—— (1956), The Recovery of Childhood Memories in Psychoanalysis. *The Psychoanalytic Study of the Child*, 11:54-88.

LAMPL-DE GROOT, J. (1967), On Obstacles Standing in the Way of Psychoanalytic Cure. *The Psychoanalytic Study of the Child*, 22:20-35.

LEWIN, B. D. & ROSS, H. (1960), *Psychoanalytic Education in the United States*. New York: Norton.

LICHTENSTEIN, E., see KALES, A.

LIPTON, R. C., see PROVENCE, S.

LOEWENSTEIN, R. M. (1954), Some Remarks on Defences, Autonomous Ego and Psycho-Analytic Technique. *Int. J. Psycho-Anal.*, 35:188-193.

McCOLLUM, A. T., see RITVO, S.

MAHLER, M. S. (1963), Thoughts about Development and Individuation. *The Psychoanalytic Study of the Child*, 18:307-324.

—— (1968), *On Human Symbiosis and the Vicissitudes of Individuation*. New York: International Universities Press.

MASTERS, W. H. & JOHNSON, V. E. (1966), *Human Sexual Response*. Boston: Little, Brown.

NAGERA, H. (1966), *Early Childhood Disturbances, the Infantile Neurosis, and the Adult Disturbances*. New York: International Universities Press.

—— ET AL., ed. (1969), *Basic Psychoanalytic Concepts on the Libido Theory* [The Hampstead Clinic Psychoanalytic Library, Vol. I]. London: George Allen & Unwin; New York: Basic Books.

OMWAKE, E., see RITVO, S.

PAVENSTEDT, E. (1966), Some Characteristics and Needs of Children Two-and-a-Half to Five. In: *On Rearing Infants and Young Children in Institutions*, ed. H. L. Witmer.

Washington: U.S. Dept. of H.E.W., Children's Bureau Research Reports, No. 1, 1967, pp. 13-20.

PROVENCE, S. & LIPTON, R. C. (1962), *Infants in Institutions.* New York: International Universities Press.

——— see also RITVO, S.

RANGELL, L. (1967), The Metapsychology of Psychic Trauma. In: *Psychic Trauma*, ed. S. S. Furst. New York: Basic Books, pp. 51-84.

RAPAPORT, D. & GILL, M. M. (1959), The Points of View and Assumptions of Metapsychology. *Int. J. Psycho-Anal.*, 40: 153-162.

REPORT of the Ad Hoc Committee on Scientific Activities, Heinz Kohut (Chairman), to the Executive Council of the American Psychoanalytic Association, December, 1967. *See also* Kohut (1970).

RITVO, S., McCOLLUM, A. T., OMWAKE, E., PROVENCE, S., & SOLNIT, A. J. (1963), Some Relations of Constitution, Environment, and Personality as Observed in a Longitudinal Study of Child Development. In: *Modern Perspectives in Child Development*, ed. A. J. Solnit & S. Provence. New York: International Universities Press, pp. 107-143.

ROBERTSON, JAMES (1952), *A Two-Year-Old Goes to Hospital* [16 mm. film]. London: Tavistock Institute of Human Relations; New York: New York University Film Library.

——— (1958), *Going to Hospital with Mother* [16 mm. film]. London: Tavistock Institute of Human Relations; New York: New York University Film Library.

——— & ROBERTSON, JOYCE (1967), *Kate, Two Years Five Months, in Foster Care for Twenty-Seven Days* [16 mm. film]. London: Tavistock Institute of Human Relations; New York: New York University Film Library.

——— ——— (1968), *Jane, Seventeen Months, in Foster Care for Ten Days* [16 mm. film]. London: Tavistock Institute of Human Relations; New York: New York University Film Library.

——— ——— (1969), *John, Seventeen Months: Nine Days in a Residential Nursery* [16 mm. film]. London: Tavistock Institute of Human Relations; New York: New York University Film Library.

———— ———— (not released), *Tom, a Legless Child Reared in a Normal Group* [16 mm. film].

ROBERTSON, JOYCE, *see* ROBERTSON, JAMES

ROBINSON, H. (1966), A Proposed Day Care Experiment and Its Physical Plant. In: *On Rearing Infants and Young Children in Institutions,* ed. H. L. Witmer. Washington: U.S. Dept. of H.E.W., Children's Bureau Research Reports, No. 1, 1967, pp. 40-45.

ROSENFELD, H. (1965), *Psychotic States.* New York: International Universities Press; London: Hogarth Press.

ROSS, H., *see* LEWIN, B. D.

SADGER, J. (1921), *Die Lehre von den Geschlechtsverirrungen auf psychoanalytischer Grundlage.* Vienna: Deuticke.

SANDLER, J. (1967), Trauma, Strain, and Development. In: *Psychic Trauma,* ed. S. S. Furst. New York: Basic Books, pp. 154-174.

SCHWARTZ, R. D., *see* DONNELLY, R. C.

SENN, M. J., E. & SOLNIT, A. J. (1968), *Problems in Child Behavior and Development.* Philadelphia: Lea & Febiger.

SOLNIT, A. J., *see* RITVO, S., *and* SENN, M. J. E.

SPITZ, R. A. (1945), Hospitalism. *The Psychoanalytic Study of the Child,* 1:53-74.

———— (1956), Transference: The Analytical Setting and Its Prototype. *Int. J. Psycho-Anal.,* 37:380-385.

———— (1957), *Die Entstehung der ersten Objektbeziehungen.* Stuttgart: Klett.

———— (1959), *A Genetic Field Theory of Ego Formation.* New York: International Universities Press.

———— & COBLINER, W. G. (1965), *The First Year of Life.* New York: International Universities Press.

———— & WOLF, K. M. (1946a), Anaclitic Depression. *The Psychoanalytic Study of the Child,* 2:313-342.

———— ———— (1946b), The Smiling Response. *Genet. Psychol. Monogr.,* 34:57-125.

STAUB, H., *see* ALEXANDER, F.

STRACHEY, J. (1934), The Nature of the Therapeutic Action of Psycho-Analysis. *Int. J. Psycho-Anal.*, 15:127-159.

——— (1937), [Contribution to] Symposium on The Theory of the Therapeutic Results of Psycho-Analysis. *Int. J. Psycho-Anal.*, 18:139-145.

——— (1964), Editor's Note [to Analysis Terminable and Interminable (Freud, 1937)]. *Standard Edition*, 23:211-215.

TYNES, H. (1966), A Residential Nursery for Very Young Babies. In: *On Rearing Infants and Young Children in Institutions*, ed. H. L. Witmer. Washington: U.S. Dept. of H.E.W., Children's Bureau Research Reports, No. 1, 1967, pp. 23-28.

WAELDER, R. (1967), Trauma and the Variety of Extraordinary Challenges. In: *Psychic Trauma*, ed. S. S. Furst. New York: Basic Books, pp. 221-234.

WINNICOTT, D. W. (1958), *Collected Papers*. New York: Basic Books.

——— (1965), *The Maturational Processes and the Facilitating Environment*. New York: International Universities Press.

WOLF, K. M., *see* SPITZ, R. A.

ZIMMERMANN, R. R., *see* HARLOW, H. F.

Index

291